Defining the Situation

The Organization of Meaning
in Social Interaction

Defining the Situation

The Organization of Meaning
in Social Interaction

PETER McHUGH

Herbert H. Lehman College
of the
City University of New York

THE BOBBS-MERRILL COMPANY, INC.
Indianapolis and New York

Robert McGinnis
Cornell University
CONSULTING EDITOR

Contents

I

Introduction

This is a study of the "definition of the situation"—how it may arise, change, and dissolve. Although it is an old idea in sociology, the definition of the situation has usually been taken for granted as a subject of study. Like a faceless bureaucrat, it has been made to work hard; yet it is without much substance as something in its own right.

The work reported here thus starts by asking, first, how such a phenomenon as the definition of the situation is possible; and second, what happens to social interaction when the definition fails?

In regard to the first question, let me suggest that a definition is possible only when phsyical space and chronological time are transformed into social space and social time. Concerning the second question, I suggest that failure of definition will cause failure of interaction. In other words, certain dimensions of social time and social space are necessary components of the definition of the situation, and the definition of the situation is in turn a necessary component of orderly social interaction.

These ideas, much elaborated below, are tested in a laboratory setting devised to make it both easy and difficult to construct, change, and dissolve definitions of the situation. Subjects build their definitions and then are faced with a challenge to them. The challenge is resolved in some cases and not resolved in others, with the result that some definitions continue, some change, and some dissolve.

Before turning directly to our particular formulation of the definition of the situation, I will set the work in context and examine some fundamental sociological considerations. These considerations are that defining the situation serves any theoretical interest in the operation of society and any methodological interest in the observation of society. I will argue with regard to theory that a society cannot be conceived to be socially organized without reference to the experiences of members, and that the definition of the situation is a way of depicting those experiences. I will also argue that the activity of defining a situation is an *observable* and hence methodologically necessary display of the various abstractions that generally pass for the workings of society.

After an examination of these premises in the next chapter, which for many will not contain much that is new, I will proceed with a specific formulation of the definition of the situation. This will be an account of how discrete physical events are defined as real according to their own distinctively social logic of time and space—how they are transitory and enduring, constructed and annulled—while at the same time they are not so evanescent as to be indescribable.

A remark about the use of italic in this book. This was not done out of rage or innocence, even when it smacks of hyperbole. It just didn't seem possible to point up certain important matters by adopting a *New York Times* stance of the ultimate reasonableness of things.

My indebtedness to the writings of Harold Garfinkel is very great. Without in any way holding him responsible for what is to follow, it can be said that his influence will be seen by even the most casual reader. I want also to thank Aaron V. Cicourel, Alan F. Blum, Jack Douglas, Scott Greer, Raymond W. Mack, John Meyer, Marvin B. Scott, and Ralph H. Turner for their helpful suggestions.

II

Defining
the Situation
and the Traditions
of Sociology

Posing the problem of social order has become a tradition in the study of social life. It asks how we can account for our observation that human behavior is usually organized and concerted rather than random, and the answer varies from theorist to theorist. Thomas Hobbes, one of the first to pose this question explicitly, suggests that people realize the likelihood of war, each against all, if they do not forego the vagaries of pure individualism, and so they rationally turn to the state for protection against that realization.[1] Emile Durkheim and Talcott Parsons share with Hobbes the importance of his question, but they object to his answer. They believe that society inculcates a set of rules and behaviors enforced less by individual will and political sovereignty than by the independent preexistence of society itself. Durkheim and Parsons transform the state into society.[2]

These macrocosmic views of social order differ substantially from the view that emphasizes the dynamics of social interaction on a smaller scale. George Herbert Mead, John Dewey, Alfred Schutz, and W. I. Thomas, among others, answer the problem of order with a discussion of such processes as role-taking and definition of the situation.[3] Thomas'

---

[1] Thomas Hobbes, *The Leviathan* (London: J.M. Dent and Sons, 1928), p. 6.

[2] Emile Durkheim, *On the Division of Labor in Society*, trans. by George Simpson (New York: The Macmillan Company, 1933). Parsons' earliest complete statement of this position appears in *The Structure of Social Action* (Glencoe, Ill.: The Free Press. 1949), pp. 77-82.

[3] George Herbert Mead, *Mind, Self and Society*, Charles W. Morris, ed. (Chicago: The University of Chicago Press, 1934); John Dewey, *Experience and Nature* (Chicago: Open Court, 1926); Alfred Schutz, *Collected Papers*, Vols. I and II (The Hague: Martinus Nijhoff, 1962); W. I. Thomas, *Social Behavior and Personality*, Edmond H. Volkhart, ed. (New York: Social Science Research Council, 1951). "If men define situations as real, they are real in their consequences" originally appeared in W. I. Thomas, *The Child in America* (New York: Knopf, 1928, p. 584).

famous aphorism, "If men define situations as real, they are real in their consequences," led workers in this tradition to investigate how persons develop common perspectives and communicate these perspectives to one another. They observe order and want to know why, just as Hobbes, Durkheim, and Parsons do. But they build their answers from the ground up rather than from the top down. They imply, by their use of the phrase "definition of the situation," that there is no one-to-one correspondence between an objectively real world and people's perspectives of that world, that instead something intervenes when events and persons come together, an intervention that makes possible the variety of interpretations which Schutz calls "multiple realities."[4] According to this view, the same events or objects can have different meanings for different people, and the degree of difference will produce comparable differences in behavior. Long a sticky issue in philosophy, the epistemology of variable meaning need not directly concern us here, because we are not interested in how man can logically justify what he does so much as we are interested in how he goes about doing what he does.[5] We need only look around us to see people acting in concert; they apparently come to adopt compatible definitions of their situations, the principle of variable meaning notwithstanding. By the same token, however, we also see people acting differently in similar situations. Why? Society, it is said, provides a baseline of interpretation for its members. But it remains to be seen just what mechanisms are operating to determine those interpretations at the point where they are actually being constructed.

These "higher" levels of analysis are incomplete because they ignore the interpenetration of society and interaction. They do not in themselves describe how the mundane activities of ordinary members can be

---

[4] Alfred Schutz, "On Multiple Realities," reprinted in *Collected Papers, I: The Problem of Social Reality* (The Hague: Martinus Nijhoff, 1962), pp. 207-259. It is the general tautological case that an event which is not part of a "system" must be assimilated by it to some degree before it can be a cause of action in that system, that is, to be part of a system requires being part of that system. The special point here, however, is that some single event, as described by its location in physical space and chronological time, need not be a single event as described by social actors. The question for us thus becomes how are we to conceptualize the way some single event can become a multiple of itself.

[5] Philosophers' growing interest in the analysis of ordinary language, by which they mean analysis of the language as it is used by ordinary people, represents their acceptance of this aspect of meaning.

conceived as maintaining or changing what happens at the very general levels of society, although these mundane activities are the vehicles of society. To suggest that society is "exterior" to interaction is only to say that society is not a carbon copy of mind,[6] but it is not to say that society is not experienced by members or that society does not depend for its continued existence upon a membership that interacts. If society were so exterior that it could not be experienced, the discipline of sociology would be impossible. Suicide, as disjuncture between member and society, would never be taken as an appropriate topic. Nor would alienation, which is a specific description of members' experiences. Macrosocial ideas and analyses are in this respect insufficient because both society and interaction are preconditions of one another, and to have social order at a societal level there must be some (not necessarily identical) order at the interactional level.

Because our statements about society and order ultimately rest upon the activities of members, we must make problematic the relationship between macroscopic properties such as "culture" and the experiential properties by which they can be said to operate. To fully describe an institution as a locus of group rules, for example, requires some description of how the institution looks to those engaging in the action, because they will act according to how it looks to them, and in so doing the institution will be maintained or changed.[7]

An example of this is the idea of "false consciousness." One way, an experiential way, of describing behavior and norms is by discerning to which groups in society one aspires and to which he believes he belongs. Upon discovering these, we are sometimes led to assert that our aspirations can be "wrong" or inappropriate, that is, false. But false by what standards? To say false is not to deny the experience of identity, but to characterize it. It is false not in the sense that it does not exist, but be-

---

[6] By mind I mean only that members refer to things and can articulate a future, not that there is a ghost in the machine, free will, or individual determination of society. *See* Gilbert Ryle, *The Concept of Mind* (New York: Barnes and Noble, 1949); Peter Strawson, *Individuals* (New York: Doubleday, 1963); J.L. Austin, "Other Minds," in Anthony Flew, ed., *Logic and Language* (New York: Doubleday, 1965), pp. 342-380.

[7] This is not a reference to intended and unintended consequences, but to the general institutional effects of varieties of interaction in varieties of conditions by varieties of members, whatever their intentions. *See* the discussion to follow of "false consciousness."

cause it is out of accord with some imposed standard that utilizes society and institutions as the important criteria of truth. It is certainly not false in the way a breach of some chess rule would be false, or in the way calling someone by the wrong name would be wrong. Nevertheless, it becomes a short step to denote society as objective and experience as subjective.

Like Hegel and Adam Smith, Marx ascribed meanings to the process of social interactions. Adam Smith's 'unseen hand' and Hegel's 'ruse of the idea,' appear in Marx's system as an objective logic of dynamic institutions that work themselves out behind the backs of the actors. In so far as men know not what they do, they realize the blind forces of society. Although these forces are the work of men, they simply remain, in Veblen's term, 'opaque.' Thus Marx measures the subjective notions of the actors of the system against the objective meaning as revealed by scientific study. And in the comparison and typical incongruity between what men think they do and the objective social functions of their acts, Marx locates the ideological nature of the subject's 'false consciousness.'[8]

Now the issue here is not whether man's purposes inevitably come to pass. Of course they don't. It is rather what we are to take as the purport of "men know not what they do." At the moment of doing, they must "know" what they are doing if by that we mean they are defining what they are doing, unless we deny that men can be said to be conscious (aware, responsive), an assertion that neither Hegel nor Marx nor a conditioning table would make.[9] But how do they know? By using some rule or criterion in some situation. And how can they be wrong? By applying some other rule or criterion. To say "false consciousness" is to re-

---

[8] H. H. Gerth and C. Wright Mills, *From Max Weber* (New York: Oxford, 1959), p. 58.

[9] In one sense, Marx adopted the viewpoint expressed here in statements like "consciousness can never be anything else than conscious existence, and the existence of men is their *actual life process.*" (italics supplied.) It is probably not a distortion to equate the phrase "actual life process" with experience. Then Marx adds that consciousness is "emancipated" into a deranged superstructure as a result of the division of labor. But it is still consciousness based on the actual life process (the division of labor), the difference being in the division of labor and not consciousness. The two correspond empirically—it is their *justification* that brings in the notions of subjectivity and objectivity. Karl Marx and Friedrich Engels, *The German Ideology*, ed. with an Introduction by R. Pascal (New York: International Publishers, 1960), p. 14 and *passim*.

place one criterion (common-sense) with another (institutions according to sociology). All well and good, except that it is unreasonable to ascribe *subjectivity* to one and *objectivity* to another, since both are objective in their own terms—it is the relation between the two criteria that is disjunctive.

This is not to say that the standards of the actor are always right. Indeed they may never be right according to some criterion. It is only to say that the standards of the actor, his way of making definitions, are the bases of action, and that actions are the analytic bases of institutions. An institution must in some way be experienced to continue or change, and thus an institution can be said to exist at the level of interaction. Further, interaction *must* occur before the institution can be said to exist at all, even for its own sake, and in its own macroscopic terms. Being conceptually interdependent on the one hand, and directly observable only in social action on the other, we must understand action before we can methodologically be said to have observed institutions; and an understanding of action will also provide an understanding of the institutions embedded there. The existence of each level is a condition for the existence of the other, and so, if we know about one we will also know about the other.

Thus, the relation between definition and institution poses no ineluctable paradox. Accordingly, we can ask how members can be said to be conscious, if by that we mean defining their situations. We need to describe how members define their situations, how objects are meaningful, and how that meaning shifts over the course of one's association with those objects.

Generally, then, what sociologists say about grand matters of great scale depends for its cogency on behavior at the level of social interaction. This is one of many reasons for suggesting that the definition of the situation should be examined. At the level of social interaction people are experiencing the grand matters in a way that makes those matters contingent upon the quality of that experience, there being a relation between the grand matters and the experience grandly described. The idea of the definition of the situation can help us to depict what experiencing is like and can thus serve both in its own stead and as a behavioral and methodological device to account for the relation between great matters grandly put and the prosaic details of everyday life, upon which any cosmos logically depends. Granted the preexistence of society as an abstraction. But how does this abstraction enter into the daily lives of individuals whose definitions are continually being made and remade? What are the components of the definition of the situation itself?

It would seem that those who are supposed to be dealing more regularly with the definition of the situation are symbolic interactionists, but they usually presuppose these components. We shall discuss this perspective more thoroughly later. It will suffice for now to note that in symbolic interaction a definition occurs by having taken the role of the other or by adopting a group standpoint. In so doing, one learns what is expected of him; that is, he constructs his definition of the situation:

> Fundamentally, group action takes the form of a fitting together of individual lines of action. Each individual aligns his action to the actions of others by ascertaining what they are doing or what they intend to do —that is, by getting the meaning of their acts. For Mead, this is done by the individual "taking the role" of others—either the role of a specific person or the role of a group (Mead's "generalized other"). In taking such roles the individual seeks to ascertain the intention or direction of the acts of others. He forms and aligns his own action on the basis of such interpretation of the acts of others. This is the fundamental way in which group action takes place in human society.[10]

But how *do* they take the role of the other and so "ascertain what they are doing"? What are the devices of social interpretation that make this possible and allow interaction to proceed?[11] This is not to ask, as several have, for a classification of roles to be taken on (reference groups, standpoints, and the like), but to ask how *any* role is taken on, regardless of the group of reference or standpoint chosen? Without an answer to this question, the idea of the definition of the situation will not

---

[10] Herbert Blumer, "Society as Symbolic Interaction," in Arnold M. Rose, ed., *Human Behavior and Social Processes* (Boston: Houghton Mifflin, 1962), p. 184.

[11] As a matter of fact, Robert K. Merton suggests that any serious functional analysis (which are often in the macrocosmic tradition) *must* include a description of "the *meanings* (or cognitive and affective significance) of the activity of pattern for members of the group" if the analysis is to make sense. *See* his *Social Theory and Social Structure*, rev. and enl. (Glencoe, Ill.: The Free Press, 1957), p. 56. For another statement of this position, *see* Hugh Dalziel Duncan, *Communication and the Social Order* (New Jersey: Bedminster, 1962), esp. pp. xv-xxx, 109-114, and 431-438. It should be noted, that Duncan, with very broad purpose, takes art and artistic symbolism as the consummate measure of social order. This work differs from Duncan's at least because it does not use the dramatic or artistic metaphors, and from Merton's because it avoids the concept role as an "explanation" of definition.

help us to understand how interaction takes place, except as a plausible assertion, bolstered by belief rather than evidence.

On the basis of this very brief summary of two traditional ideas in sociology, I want to suggest more directly how those ideas generate certain issues with regard to the definition of the situation.

I shall do this by immediately asserting that rules (norms, values) are a means by which society and definition can be said to coexist, because rules inhabit both the collective conscience and the member's definition. Rules are socially organized in the most encompassing sense of the term. (I am not going to justify this assertion except by appeal to the authority of the literature.)

Next, I shall draw on analytic philosophy to delineate these issues and then review several relevant works that are expressions of them. I have chosen analytic philosophy and particular sociological studies that I feel offer the most cogent descriptions of the problematic relation between rules and activity, and, therefore, the most adequate current starting points for connecting the definition of the situation and the problem of order. I might add that by issue I mean in need of description.

These issues evolve around the ideas of rules, rule-governed behavior, and the observation and description of these ideas.[12]

1. In what sense do rules "determine" definition?

Does a rule, because it can be said to exist on a societal level, automatically engender conformity at the level of interaction? "Obeying a rule" may be a practice, but is it inevitable? If not, "following a rule" becomes problematic and *needs to be investigated.* How can it be said that a rule is followed, obeyed? How is it that the rule of monogamy *is* followed, since it might not be? By this I do not mean that we should explain the following of a rule by reference to something else, say socialization. I mean we should *describe* the activity of following a rule in the way it is

---

[12] I am especially indebted here to Wittgenstein, of course, and to Cavell and Waismann. *See* Ludwig Wittgenstein, *The Blue and Brown Books* (New York: Harper and Row, 1965) ; *Philosophical Investigations,* trans. by G.E.M. Anscombe (New York: Macmillan, 1953) ; Stanley Cavell, "The Availability of Wittgenstein's Later Philosophy," in George Pitcher, ed., *Wittgenstein: The Philosophical Investigations* (New York: Doubleday and Co., 1966) ; Friedrich Waismann, "Verifiability" and "Language Strata," in Antony Flew, ed., *Logic and Language, First and Second Series* (New York: Doubleday and Co., 1965). I have used the analytic philosophers here because they pose the problems in their strongest form, and thus any solution would be the strongest solution. But I make no claim to solution, only to addressing the problems.

followed as it is being followed. A rule, for example, can be misinter-
preted in the course of being followed—a member can be incompetent
with regard to a rule. Perhaps the rule of monogamy is conceived to be
an entirely legalistic one, without exclusive rights of sexual access. Or
rules can be disobeyed, in the sense that some who know and are capable of
applying them may not do so. Access rights may be ignored. Thus, what
sorts of *observations* can we generate in order to describe the problematic
relation between general rules and the action of defining the situation?

    2. Are rules complete?

If we start out to describe the definition of the situation, and if we use
the idea of rules in so doing, will we accomplish such a description? Or
would some matters of definition be omitted, because the concrete activity
of defining extends beyond the contents which develop from rules? Perhaps defining situations is a stratum of life with its own logic, a logic that
requires something other than a description in terms of rules. Rules, for
example, may or may not be complete. Now even to ask whether or not
rules are complete is to imply that some things we want to depict may not
be covered, and not covered in the sense that rules are irrelevant rather
than missing. To begin by limiting the definition of the situation to the
occasions when rules are complete could limit a description of defining
the situation so narrowly as to obviate our purpose.

    3. Are rules an exact calculus?

Are ambiguities, troubles, vagueness, and misinterpretation as they are
because those involved "don't know their real definition, or because there
is no real 'definition' to them"?[13] In a way, this is to ask if societal rules
can be "verified" by interactants as existing in their interactions. What
makes a proof convincing? Does a proof make a proof? Do we *decide* by
calculating or do we *accept* by having been convinced? Is a definition a
mere choice, like choosing between a penny and a dollar, or is it a con-
viction? When we ask "Is it love?" do we test it by consulting some definition as if it were a proof, or are we convinced by various tenuous
evidences that could never be redeemed by an explicitly calculable and
determinant rule?

    4. What is the observable logic of the definition of the situation?

Does it have its own motif, or is it a repetition of socialization, internali-
zation, and institutionalization? Is it "bedrock" in the sense that it cannot
be fully described by anything else, say by the coming together of per-

---

[13] Wittgenstein, *The Blue and Brown Books*, p. 25.

sonalities, norms, and social structure? How does it look for its own sake, before being explained away from outside? This is to ask not for explanation, but for description.

"Why did the Puritans persecute bachelors?" is not the same query as "How did the Puritans persecute bachelors?" The first may receive an answer in terms of slavish pursuit of Biblical injunctions, of the motives of a set of women, of views about maintaining the numbers of true believers, or of the survival of a useless practice. Whichever answer is given, it will not be an answer to the second question. It will not tell us whether Puritans taxed bachelors heavily, placed them in stocks, or disenfranchised them. And this distinction between the reasons for an action or the occurrence of an event, on the one hand, and the means in which it was done or the way it took place, on the other hand, is what in the present connection we refer to by the words "explanation" and "description" respectively.[14]

What I shall do now is take several kinds of work that are closely related to the problem of order, rules, and the definition of the situation, and briefly assess them in terms of these issues.

In Talcott Parsons' work, the social order consists in part in the translation of cultural values into social norms, which become the rules by which behavior is governed at the level of interaction.

The logical starting point for analysis of the role of normative elements in human action is the fact of experience that men not only respond to stimuli, but in some sense try to conform their action to patterns which are, by the actor and by members of the same collectivity, deemed desirable. The statement that this is a fact, like all statements of fact, involves a conceptual scheme. The most fundamental component of that scheme is what is here called the means-end scheme. . . . There is no such thing as action except as effort to conform with norms.[15]

Norms become concrete means and ends of action and a source of identity between member and system. The social order resides in this identity. Norms are a source of identity because they diminish the potential distinction between self and collectivity, since they engender a coinciding interest for the self and for the collectivity. Through this identity persons are committed to the social system—they can be called members

---

[14] Robert Brown, *Explanation in Social Science* (Chicago: Aldine Publishing Co. 1963), p. 20.
[15] Parsons, *The Structure of Social Action*, p. 76.

—and thus their behaviors cohere. Norms establish the ground rules, and a social system is stable when these norms are effective in governing interaction.

The question here is, what are the *actual* ways in which members go about their ends and means? What does an action look like with regard to the *concrete observables* that would *describe* for us the activity proposed as rule-governed? Because it is at least possible that a rule may not be obeyed, government needs to be pictured for us. How are norms invoked during interaction, what does obeying a rule look like concretely? Does it come out universalism just like that, ensconced in abstraction? In what sense can norms be said to "appear"? The action scheme is metaphorical, because we are without a reproducible description of the *actual activity* which is supposed to be "explained" by the notion that norms are followed by men. If a rule can be followed or not, then the *way* it is followed or not becomes our descriptive task. We cannot, of course, say we have explained anything that has not been described. All we know by having consulted the action scheme is what we have already posed as issues: Rules can be followed or not, they may or may not be complete, they may or may not be exact, definition may or may not have its own logic. Parsons suggests that rules *can* be followed, and provides us with units in which rules *might* be followed, but we are without a description of the ways rules *are* followed.

Alfred Schutz advanced the empirical idea of norms one step by talking about them *as they are formulated by the actor*. A philosopher, Schutz is typically treated as though he were only a theorist, but his version of the attitude of everyday life also moves toward making norms observable. Rather than treating norms as the abstractions of the investigator, he extends them to those being observed (although they remain quite abstract). He takes them out of the sociologist and puts them into action, as something that can be watched rather than presupposed. Now, being something which actors themselves will recognize, we might be able to observe norms *among* rather than just impose them on the actors. In so doing, he moves them from the sociologist's stratum of meaning to the actor's.

> The world . . . is from the outset experienced in the pre-scientific thinking of everyday life in the mode of typicality . . . and depends upon my practical or theoretical "problem at hand." Thus, typification depends upon my problem at hand for the definition and solution of which the type has been formed. Typified patterns of the Others' behavior become in turn motives of my own actions, and this leads to the phenom-

enon of self-typification well known to social scientists under various names.[16]

But problems remain. If rules and typification of the problem at hand are not followed in some cases, we are left without much to say about the ways in which they are not followed (if we are permitted to say that things will "break down," this is an effect rather than a description of not following; and we are still without a description of what breaking down looks like). Further, the rules are still too abstract. They have been put above the heads of actors but not in their mouths. Schutz has reconstructed the idea of rules so as to make them potentially observable, but the actual ways in which rules are invoked remain obscure. Little is said about how these rules are *practiced.* Describing rules as assumptions that actors make is to move a step toward description of definition, because it is now *possible* that an actor will *use* them in ways that can be observed. But just how *do* assumptions get invoked *during* an interaction? Schutz has left us with a limited program for describing behavior.

Garfinkel moves forward a notch by distinguishing rules that are necessary for order (constitutive rules). Constitutive rules are necessary in the sense that a stable order requires their presence. He indicates empirically that these rules are important by violating them and then observing the disorganization that results. Garfinkel capitalizes on constituent properties of rules, and in this is directly involved with the social order, because he relates a property of social order to a property of rules.

With regard to the constitutive order of events, "It is our perennial task to locate and define the features of their situations that persons, while unaware of, are nevertheless responsive to as *required* features."[17] The fact that persons are "unaware" has an important empirical consequence because they will not appear in just any orderly circumstance and thus cannot be observed there. But because persons are "responsive" we can still have a program for observing these rules.

Our task is to learn what it takes to produce for members of a group that has stable features perceived environments that are "specifically senseless." . . . Events which are perceived by group members as being

16 Alfred Schutz, "Concept and Theory Formation in the Social Sciences," *Collected Papers,* Vol. I, p. 60.

17 Harold Garfinkel, "Conception of and Experiments with 'Trust' as a Condition of Stable Concerted Actions," in O. J. Harvey, ed., *Motivation and Social Interaction* (New York: The Ronald Press Company, 1963), p. 192.

atypical, causally indeterminate, without a relevant history or future, means character, or moral necessity.[18]

That is, we can locate and define required features by breaching them. In such a program, however, two aspects of the definition of the situation are omitted: First, we are without a description of the operation of unrequired features (preferential rules); second, we are without the possibility of a description of orderly interaction, because the program requires that "we produce perceived environments which are specifically senseless," that is, disorderly environments.

Garfinkel does not depict for us the whole round of rule-governed activity, because he has chosen to concentrate on constitutive rules to the exclusion of those "alternatives that are treated as within the player's discretion to comply with."[19] Now, if rules are invoked as situations are defined, and if rules are both constitutive and preferential, we must incorporate preferential rules to describe the definition of the situation. We need the contingent as well as necessary rules by which something comes to be meaningful. Having long hair may not be a constitutive property of "woman," but it can be a part of being a woman in the sense that it makes a difference to those around her. We want to locate and define the *symptoms* of membership and not just the essential criteria of membership—meanings which actors treat as matters of interest even though they do not stand as bona fides. We want to do this because, as an element of social order, defining the situation is a bedrock "form of life."[20] Therefore it is necessary to *describe* it rather than explain it by showing how it exhibits features external to itself. It is in this sense that the exclusion of preferential rules makes any such statement about defining the situation a metaphorical one. Being bedrock, it must be fully described, but cannot be without utilizing the preferential as well as constitutive property of rules. And being bedrock, orderly definition must be described as well, because we are no longer using definition to delineate anything except itself.

I am asking here whether the definition of the situation can be described, not by going outside of itself—not by calling it determined by

---

[18] *Ibid.*, p. 189. It should be said here that Garfinkel has recently moved away from this position. *See* his *Studies in Ethnomethodology* (New York: Prentice-Hall, 1967).

[19] *Ibid.*, p. 192.

[20] Wittgenstein, *Philosophical Investigations*, p. 226 and *passim*.

constitutive rules, or socialization, or social structure—but according to its own motif. What sort of logic does it represent, not how is it caused? What are its internal relations, not what effect does it have?

A man who writes aphorisms may say a thing, and, on another occasion, the very opposite of it without being guilty of a contradiction. Each aphorism, as it stands, is quite complete in itself. Two different aphorisms are not parts of one and the same communication. Suppose you go to a museum where several paintings are hung on the wall. Would you complain that they are not correlated and do not fit into one and the same perspective? Well now, each painting has a pictorial space of its own. What is represented in two paintings, though the paintings may be adjacent, is not in the same pictorial space. It is the first aim of Art, it has been said, to set a frame around Nature. Sometimes the frame is large, sometimes small, but it is always there. An aphorism is Literature and done with ink instead of colors. Of two aphorisms each is in a frame of its own. Hence no clash. . . . No: seeming contradictions are not always absurd.[21]

An aphorism or painting is a puzzle only when it is presumed that it must be causing, or caused by, or related to something external to itself. Only then can it be contradictory, and we could not arrive at such a conclusion until after describing it for its own sake, without referring to some external criterion of logic. By the same token, the definition of the situation deserves to be so described. Perhaps actors are "unaware," but why not describe this unawareness? What does it mean, by way of description, to say that actors are unaware?

This is not so metaphysical as it seems if by bedrock we mean some content which helps solve the problem of a discipline—in sociology if it *connects with the problem of social order*. It is then not to be explained by some other notion, but rather only to be described because it *is* an element of social order and requires no further justification. It is in this sense a form of life, a rendering of an event that needs no further grounds. To explain a form of life in terms of something else is to revise the question it was intended to answer, with the result that the description is not the same answer either. One is playing a different game.

What I now suggest we do—and this is a programme for the future —is to reverse the whole situation by saying: "The formal motifs which we have been considering all combine to impress a certain stamp on a

---

21 Waismann, "Language Strata," p. 238.

stratum; they give us the means to characterize each stratum 'from within,' that is, with no reference to the subject." If we carefully study the texture of the concepts which occur in a given stratum, the logic of its propositions, the meaning of truth, the web of verification, the sense in which a description may be complete or incomplete—if we consider all that, we may thereby characterize its subject-matter.[22]

Summary

This brief description of the history and issues in the problem of order suggests the basic question guiding the research reported here. We want to know how men define things as real. To the degree that the way men define things makes a difference, and to the degree that some kind of definition must take place if there is to be social action, then a description of definition is a description of one of the elements of social order.

We shall go about this by describing how a definition comes to be so given the existence of perspectives already determined by society, culture, and reference group. It is a study of the devices by which meaning is assigned or not, rules are invoked or not, actors are made aware or not, from which flows the substance and content of any particular interaction. Because all theories presuppose these devices, I suggest that making them explicit and observable will generally improve sociological knowledge.

---

[22] *Ibid.*, p. 246.

III

Parameters of Definition: Members' "Knowledge" Through Time and Space

We shall use the terms "emergence" and "relativity" rather extensively, even though they are not very familiar except as metaphors.[1] Before attempting a definition, perhaps we should see how they have been used. According to Mead, emergence and relativity are bases of knowledge, and knowledge is the basis of any human endeavor. In the pragmatic tradition, knowledge is not equated with a mechanical cause-effect criterion by which truth is separated from falsity, but rather with any "fact" from which one infers the existence of something else.[2] That fact may be scientific, metaphysical, or merely metaphorical; the one making the inference may be scientist, shaman, or the world's most average man. It is what members believe to be true in that they base their actions upon it. Knowledge in this sense thus includes concrete information, rules, social norms—anything that gives meaning to an observation (making a "self" the knowledge of an object that is also the subject). These are all forms of knowledge that depict for the actor all the possible events in which he assumes he may participate.

The critical point is that emergence and relativity both create and limit the possibility of knowledge.[3] To the extent, then, that "knowledge"

---

[1] George Herbert Mead, *The Philosophy of the Present* (Chicago: Open Court, 1932) *passim*. See Duncan, *Communication and the Social Order*, p. 81n. for a comment on Mead's use of time and space.

[2] John Dewey, *Logic: The Theory of Inquiry* (New York: Henry Holt, 1938), p. 113. I have not addressed the way in which a "fact" is decided. See Stephen E. Toulmin, *The Uses of Argument* (Cambridge, England: Cambridge University Press, 1958), esp. the sections on warrant, pp. 94-146.

[3] Mead, *The Philosophy of the Present*, pp. 68-90.

must in some way come into play if there is to be social order, and if emergence and relativity are the conditions of "knowledge," we must account for emergence and relativity if we are to account for order. Otherwise stated, a social order of coherent knowledge would be impossible unless emergence and relativity made them so. We may now move on to an examination of the meaning of these concepts.

Emergence

Emergence concerns the temporal dimension of activity, wherein past, present, and future are analytically distinct and, at the same time, inextricable, for they are not correspondingly distinct in their influence upon concrete behavior. Things or events do occur in the chronological past, present, or future, and we can use these divisions to clarify our statements about events. But to assume that there is no metachronological influence of the one upon the other would make it impossible to account for social interaction. Take, for example, the idea of occupational achievement. A man may, at 21 years of age, make $7,500 a year in a bookkeeping job. He may at 35 make $100,000 a year as president of a firm. If he anticipates at 21 that in the future he will gain upward mobility by the time he is 35, his $7,500 will hold different meaning for him than if he expects to remain in the same job forever.[4] Similarly, after he becomes president, the past bookkeeping job has a different meaning for him (e.g., "preparation" or "the learning of work discipline") than if he had not become president (e.g., "treadmill" or "the wrong auspices"). There are chronological pasts, presents, and futures here, but their social influence upon one another transforms the purely physical metric as the course of events unfolds. This is so because the past influences the symbolic definition of the present, the definition of the present is influenced by inferences about the future, and the events of the future will reconstruct our definition of the past: "I have defined emergence as the presence of things in two or more different systems, in such a fashion that its presence in the later system changes its character in the earlier system

---

[4] Schutz, *The Problems of Social Reality*, p. 69, notes that the future perfect tense depicts the time structure of projects of action, but that no future ever turns out exactly as the future perfect had it because, at the very least, the person has grown older, which cannot be experienced ahead of time.

to which it belongs."[5] Here we have the notion of some item or thing existing in one system (the past) and in another (the future) as judged from a single point in time, and as it exists in the future it changes the character of its existence in the past. The item can be an event, like the commission of a crime; a memory, such as the recall of footnote procedures; or an attitude, such as ethnocentrism.

The interior monologue of fiction and certain recent European films (e.g., *Last Year at Marienbad*) are a nearly perfect representation of emergence, for they are devices used to indicate the influence of pasts and futures upon contemporaneous behavior, the reconstructing influence of each upon each, and the potential interplay of every single event upon every other in the life of a character or group. Here it is not the chronological sequence that is paginated seriatim, but the social sequence, where an event is described by another according to their relations to social action rather than in minutes, days, months and years. Quentin's suicide in *The Sound and the Fury* is his reconstruction of the relevant events of his past and his anticipation of what will happen to him in the future. They are intrinsic to the suicide, independently of their place according to Greenwich time. As a series of social actions, discrete physical chronology is transformed into corporate meaning. Those who feel that this genre of fiction is difficult probably do so because the chronological and social sequences of meaning are not in one-to-one correspondence with one another. Nor should they be, because the social present is formed by both the current meaning of the past and the current anticipation of the future.

Moving closer to sociology, one can depict drug addiction as a state in which the anticipated future of withdrawal continuously informs the meaning of the chronological present, and in effect *exists* in the social present because it creates the addiction of the moment. Similarly, a popular autobiography is the use of the past by a cultural hero and his audience so that they may give meaning to his exalted present; the import being not whether the past occurred as depicted, but how it is called forth to make the present meaningful. In this particular example, the autobiographical content is, itself, an aspect of the man's current esteem. A final and prosaic illustration: We have all heard stories of someone who has just missed being killed in an airplane crash. Suppose the emergent item is the "airplane ride," in that it belongs to both a later and

---

[5] Mead, *The Philosophy of the Present*, p. 69.

an earlier system. As the person is told that the airplane is full because it is oversold, the "airplane ride" assumes the character of a missed appointment in some other city (exemplifying the influence of the future on the present thwarted airplane ride). In the later system, after being told of the crash, the significance of the ride changes, because the person is now "lucky" to have escaped disaster. The meaning of the airplane ride has changed, and it is emergent because future programs influence the depiction of the present, just as the actual events that occur in the future (now the present) make it necessary to reconstruct the past, in this case from disappointment to relief for the passenger. An event is, in this sense, always becoming and never complete. It is continuously achieved and, while its influence may be suspended at one time or another, cannot be ascribed. With perhaps slight exaggeration, the meaning of a death itself shifts regularly for those concerned, whatever its biological finality.

Thus the process of emergence *is* the present, for it is the point at which all the impingements on behavior contemporaneously intersect: "That which marks the present is its becoming and its disappearing," and it is "a continual sliding . . . of passages into each other, constituted by a process whose earlier phases determine in certain respects their later phases."[6] And because our reconstructed pasts and future programs are part of emergence, so do they become part of the present.

Alfred Schutz has suggested a more specific, though faulty, relation between present and future. In depicting the common sense assumptions that guide the man on the street, he calls one such supposition the "etcetera assumption."[7] People assume that future events will occur as they have in the past, a procedure that makes it possible to routinize the environment, which in turn makes an order possible. For if this was not so, obviously, no one would be able to get out of bed and dressed in the morning; rather, he would think until bedtime of every alternative procedure and potential happenstance.

This description may be adequate as a very general statement of time and the events it orders. It remains to detail the precise features of the etcetera assumption as it operates in action, and to specify how such an assumption about time and repetition fares in the actual situations of everyday behavior. Are there not changes and unexpected events that can be assimilated by both persons and organizations which do not

---

6 *Ibid.,* p. 28.

7 Schutz, *The Problem of Social Reality,* pp. 3-47.

disrupt the order, the etcetera assumption notwithstanding? How do we manage surprise, and when are we unable to do so? In what ways are past, present, and future reciprocally constructed to form an ordered whole, and how may they be turned into a disordered number of unrelated fragments? Further, what are the social conditions of these phenomena, the kinds of relations between members, and between member and situation, in which they are likely to occur? In sociological terms, what kinds of social relations can create and frustrate the definitions of the situation which make continued interaction possible?

So much for the basic idea. To test emergence, to move beyond speculation, we must ask why the past is continually being rewritten, and then specify how this is attained. What is there in the nature of being that makes it necessary to recast the past, and, in so doing, to change the meaning of the present and future as well?

Simply put, it is because an unanticipated change in the present requires a change in the assessment of the past and anticipated future. In a causal account of an event, any unanticipated change in the character of the event requires a change in the accounting system. The development of novelty, surprise, or the unexpected is the impetus to the reconstruction of what already has happened.[8] It has been argued that in science, for example, it is the character of the accounting scheme that implicates some findings as surprising and others as expected; and that when a finding is surprising it is the accounting scheme that is modified, not the finding.[9] We shall investigate in some detail the connections between novel or surprising events and consequent shifts in the definitions of the situation—how surprise induces reconstruction (redefinition) of the past, thereby influencing a subject's definition of the present and his expectations for the future.[10] We shall also attempt to *regulate* the pro-

---

[8] Mead, *The Philosophy of The Present*, pp. 48-51. Unfortunately, Mead's references to novelty are few.

[9] Thomas Kuhn, *The Structure of Scientific Revolutions* (Chicago: University of Chicago Press, 1962).

[10] This notion of time is not particularly esoteric, although it seldom has been thoroughly examined. Parsons was among the first contemporary sociologists to refer to the temporal aspect of behavior in *The Structure of Social Action*. In the old terminology, means-ends relationships subsume some kind of *process*, and so require a consideration of passage. (In fact, any use of the term *process* is an explicit reference to time, though not necessarily chronological time.) "Action in its course," Weber's idea that underlies nearly all of Parson's formulations, implies some reciprocal influence between past, present, and future, and so falls within Mead's framework. However, Parsons did not depict process in temporal terms except to assert its existence.

cedure by changing the interactional environment of subjects, so as to illuminate *social* features of the definition of the situation.

Relativity

As emergence is temporal and involves an event in both the old and the new, relativity is spatial and characterizes an event in its relationship to other events across the boundaries of space.[11] Relativity, of course, means that there can be no absolute time and space by which a datum, and relations between data, can exist. Motion can be used as an example.

> The spatial, temporal and energic characters of objects vary with the velocity of motion in relation to the world which is at rest. . . . But the consentient set which is moving may be regarded as at rest, while its environment will then be regarded as moving with like velocity and in an opposite sense. . . . The reality of motion does not lie in the change but in the relative positions of things, regarded as events, with reference to each other.[12]

In other words, when one's own train is standing in the station and the one on the next track begins to move, it is just as legitimate to conceive of one's own train as moving and the other as at rest, because there is no absolute motionmeter standing *outside* the world as a final arbiter. Rather, there are only events and their relationships to each other, so it becomes senseless to speak of one thing as absolutely moving and the other as absolutely at rest except by definition, that is, by agreement that one will be considered to have moved and the other not to have moved.

Relativity indicates the absence of an ultimate reality; in this aspect it is similar to the notions of "misplaced concreteness" and "multiple realities."[13] *Only criteria can signify reality and criteria are variable.*

---

[11] Mead, *The Philosophy of the Present*, pp. 12, 39-46, and *passim*. His delineation is abstruse for the sociologist because it is often expressed in terms of physics.

[12] *Ibid.*, p. 39. These issues go back to Zeno. For recent work on the epistemology of time and space, see *The Philosophy of Time*, ed. Richard Gale (New York: Doubleday & Co., 1967).

[13] Alfred North Whitehead, *Science and the Modern World* (New York: The Macmillan Company, p. 75; Schutz, "On Multiple Realities," *The Problem of Social Reality*, pp. 207-259. *See also* James' discussion of whether a man chasing a squirrel around a tree can be said to go around the squirrel. According to terrestial criteria he can; according to interceptive criteria he cannot. William James, *Pragmatism* (New York: Longmans, Green and Co., 1949), pp. 43-44.

Because of the nature of conceptualization, the denotative and connotative meanings of concepts cannot fully exist except for the observer who conceptualizes. Consequently, if observations differ according to time and place of measurement, there is no possibility of a physical or social ontology. There are instead "multiple realities"—valid though varied descriptions of a set of relationships that depend upon one's perspective or location within the set.

If, for analytic purposes and at whatever risk, we neglect the notion of time, we are left with an instantaneous depiction of spatial arrangements. Because different positions make up the set, there are different perspectives. These perspectives are "standpoints,"[14] and are basic to role theory, because they are the positions of self that must be overcome, and the positions of others that must be taken on, if there is to be social meaning, concerted social intercourse, reciprocal action, that is, if there is to be social order.

We must describe how these discrete standpoints are overcome and made interchangeable. But if separate perspectives require different measurement systems, how can standpoints be interchanged? Do the different measurement systems obviate an exchange? "Can a thing with changing spatio-temporal dimensions be the same thing (yet) with different dimensions, when we have seemingly only these dimensions by which to define the thing?"[15] How do some events come to be called objective and real, whereas others are said to be subjective and phenomenal, given the reported position of relativity? Perhaps through "transformation in passage," wherein "what has taken place issues in what is taking place, and in this passage what has occurred determines spatio-temporally what is passing into the future."[16] This answer is hardly clear, however, and certainly not a solution. Mead does connect spatial perspective with the "mind" in that he says "the same passage occurs in the mind as occurs in nature."[17] Presumably, "nature" means something independent of the perspectives of humans, whereas "mind" is peculiarly human, there being an analogue between the two that allows for some transformation of per-

---

[14] Ralph H. Turner, "Role-Taking, Role Standpoint, and Reference Group Behavior," *American Journal of Sociology*, 61 (1956), pp. 316-328; Schutz, "Common-Sense and Scientific Interpretation of Human Action," *The Problem of Social Reality*, p. 11.

[15] Mead, *The Philosophy of the Present*, p. 79.

[16] *Ibid.*, p. 13.

[17] *Ibid.*, p. 80.

spective into action. Nevertheless, this is more assertion than exposition.

However, one can extrapolate a basis for overcoming the disparate spatial locations that create similarly disparate perspectives in defining a situation. If we accept rather than question the existence of a social order, if we look on observed empirical regularities as the effects of some actual, concrete ability to take the role of the other, we can for the purposes of argument ask how such a phenomenon *does* occur rather than how it *can* occur. In so doing we ask how relativity operates in social circumstances rather than how it is limited by epistemology, and this is, of course, our purpose here.

A strategy in this quest is to ask how persons use concepts. The concept has historically been considered the substance of communication, and hence the way concepts are used—their rules of use—as the vehicles by which substance is communicated and the limits of one's own position are overcome. Rules of use, as the fundamental vehicles of communication, are procedures in the sense that they contain a social methodology. Because they contain a methodology, they thus are the criteria by which meaning is assigned, decisions are made, objects are characterized—they provoke and constrain the assignment of factual status. As the criteria of factual status, they entail certain actions for the actor.

We must ask, therefore, how the use of concepts enables role-taking to occur and a semblance of common meaning to pervade everyday activity. We should briefly remind one another that we are not here interested in concepts as epistemology, or in the logic of knowledge as opposed to mere belief. Instead, we hope to investigate concepts as they are used by men in constructing definitions of situations, whether or not those definitions are composed of logic or belief, and whether or not they meet the canons of analytic philosophy. Let me suggest, following Schutz, that interactants (1) *assume* their concepts are valid descriptions of the world, (2) *assume* other interactants are using the same concepts in the same ways, and (3) practically never bother to check those assumptions.[18] (The disclaimer "practically" will be discussed below.)

The interchangeability of standpoints thus becomes dependent upon a predilection to agreement by persons on what is "real" to them as opposed to what is "illusory" to them, agreements embodied in the rules of

---

[18] Schutz, "Common-Sense and Scientific Interpretation of Human Action," *The Problem of Social Reality*, pp. 7-34; "The Dimensions of the Social World," reprinted Arvid Broderson, ed., *Collected Papers, II: Studies in Social Theory* (The Hague: Martinus Nijhoff, 1964), pp. 20-63.

use by which the situation comes to be defined. Social meaning is made possible by the contract of agreement.[19] Thus objects, whether norms, materials, deviants, or changes, can be real as opposed to illusory for the man on the street because he and others can presume to agree that such objects have entered their sensational field and are known in common. At the same time, however, the actor leaves room for the possibility that these same objects can be known for special qualities *not* held in common due to some special experience or conceptualization that falls out of the realm of the commonplace experience or concept.[20] Here the actor is aware that he has some experiences that are unshared by other partners to the interaction and fall outside the common culture, thereby making some of his perspectives private. The presumption of agreement on objects known in common is the fiat that makes interchangeability of standpoints occur, while the assumption that oneself and others can also draw private relevances from the same objects is the vagueness—the "open texture"—that makes it unnecessary to continue checking and rechecking the original fiat.[21] Vagueness is the uncertainty of usage that allows definitional latitude on one hand and definitional reappraisal on the other. This brings us back to the point that, for the social actor, alternative interpretations of any single event are quite possible. This is probably the major difference between social recipes and, say, chemical ones.

To sum up, we are attempting to describe the definition of the situation. There are two formal parameters of the definition of the situation, and changes in these parameters, of course, will manifest themselves in changes in particular concrete definitions. These parameters are emergence and relativity. Emergence refers to definition, and transformations in definition, of an event over time. Relativity refers to definition and its transformation across space. Recalling our earlier brief discussion of var-

---

19 The very idea of "culture" introduces itself as a set of agreements about how events are to be interpreted. Simmel's stranger is a man who, because he is foreign to the culture, cannot share these agreements, with the consequence that he cannot make social exchanges because "he is no owner of (cultural) soil." *The Sociology of George Simmel*, trans. by Kurt H. Wolff, ed. (Glencoe, Ill.: The Free Press, 1950), p. 403.

20 Schutz, "Common-Sense and Scientific Interpretation of Human Action," *The Problem of Social Reality*, p. 12.

21 Open texture is Waismann's term: "It is not possible to define a concept . . . with absolute precision, i.e., in such a way that every nook and cranny is blocked against entry of doubt." He distinguishes between vagueness and open texture, but we shall not. *See* Waismann, "Verifiability," in Flew, *Logic and Language*, pp. 122-151.

iable meaning, and attaching the idea to the definition of the situation, we can suggest that relationships in time and space are ways of describing the various substantive definitions that social actors construct for a specific event. Furthermore, social activity is in some way an outcome of those relationships; therefore, to account for social activity, we must account for emergence and relativity as well. But these ideas are still very general, making it incumbent upon us to specify their parts.

IV

Properties
of Emergence
and Relativity

Emergence

Remember that emergence includes, in the present, the changing meaning of past events and future programs. The *social* character of events, rather than their epistemological truth or falsity, can develop new and different features even after the event has occurred or before it happens.

Karl Mannheim has suggested that "patterned" definitions depend upon relating previous interpretations to present circumstances, a process in which the actor searches for homologies that "underlie" the behavior of the moment. It is a " . . . search for documentary meaning, for an identical, homologous pattern underlying a vast variety of totally different realizations of meaning."[1] As patterns are discovered, they are documented by the actor in his immediate, ongoing situations, thus allowing him to integrate temporally discrete events by giving them a baseline of meaning, and, thereby, to ascribe order to the general environment. Although the content of any pattern is in some way normative, the documentary method itself is independent of the normative content. It is a parameter of social life, regardless of the specific content invoked at any particular time. The documentary method is a formula used by actors to maintain temporal congruity in the environment and to keep meaning extensive in time. It is the common-sense empiric, the method used by the man on the street to homogenize temporal events.

---

[1] Karl Mannheim, "On the Interpretation of Weltanschauung," in Paul Kecskemeti, trans. and ed., *Essays on the Sociology of Knowledge* (New York: Oxford University Press, 1952), pp. 53-63.

More specifically, the search for homologous patterns uses an immediate referent as representative of (the document of) an underlying pattern. Let us use an ethnic example here. Merton, *et al.* describe the contents of two apparently contradictory normative appelations: "Becoming a doctor is worthy," and "Becoming a doctor is overly ambitious and greedy." They theoretically resolve these contradictions by a concept like status separation, in which the ethnic position of the normative object determines which depiction will be selected.[2] The question we would ask is (1) how the process of selection operates between the observation of the phenomenon (doctoring) and its characterization (as worthy or ambitious) but (2) *only as a special case of a behavioral parameter.* That is, we would like an explanation of the workings of this aspect of ethnicity that falls under the same hermeneutic rubric by which we describe, say, the process of communicating meaning through time between interviewer and respondent, husband and wife, office holder and electorate.[3]

Yet descriptions of the documentary method have been cursory. Mannheim scatters tidbits throughout an essay, "On the Interpretation of Weltanschauung," none of which contain much more information than is quoted above. Ergo,

"A datum which is apprehended as being there in its own right can, and indeed must, also be conceived as standing for something else." (p. 43)

"Documentary meaning . . . is a matter of the character, the essential nature, the "ethos" of the subject." (p. 55)

"Now after the documentary meaning of one phase is ascertained, we need still further evidence in order to make the characterization complete . . . . We have to range over all comparable realizations. In looking further, we have corroborating instances conveying the same documentary meaning in 'homologous' fashion. In the end one will gain the impression that he has derived one common documentary meaning from a wide range of objective and expressive meanings." (p. 57)

Below is an extension of these hints which describes how actors create temporal continuity in defining situations.

---

[2] *The Student Physician*, Robert K. Merton, George C. Reader, and Patricia Kendall, eds., (Cambridge: Harvard University Press, 1957).

[3] Because the documentary method is the way normative orders are invoked, its broadest relevance is to the whole process of conduct. It is an aspect, for example, of the institutionalization of authority, the content and boundaries of legal systems, production in a factory, stratification, birthrates, and so forth.

Theme. Actors assume before the fact that a pattern of meaning will be discovered in the events they observe. They are *future oriented*, in that they take it for granted they will be able to make something of what is yet to occur. They are also past oriented, in that they take it for granted that what has already occurred will inform the future. Each of these orientations folds back as an actor's description of the present. Dinner with a marriageable partner, say, is hardly comparable to dinner with an unmarriageable one.

In a study conducted by Hays and Kennedy,[4] a single subject is placed in front of a machine that looks like a cash register. On the machine are two buttons, *A* and *B*, and above them a "Predict" sign where the amount of sale would be. The subject is instructed to punch either the *A* or *B* button every time the predict sign pops up. After he does so either the *A* or *B* button will light up as an indication of the "correct" choice. The procedure is then repeated over and over, and the subject is told to try to predict the correct answer as often as he can. Unknown to him, another subject, who has been given the same instructions, is in another room facing the same kind of machine. It is the latter's predictions that light up as the original subject's correct choices and vice versa. As one subject predicts by pushing either the *A* or *B* button, this prediction appears on the other subject's machine as a "correct" choice. The great majority of these couples developed a patterned set of choices, although they were not collaborating with one another, if by collaboration we mean they consulted with one another. They did not even know that they were dealing with another person.

Our interest in this study is in the way developed patterns are themes. Let us imagine a very simple design of theme, say *ABAB*. At any single point *A*, the actor is informed as to where he is at the moment, where he will be, and where he has been, by the *whole sequence of acts*. Simply describing an *A* as an *A* does not capture the activity of these subjects, nor does it describe the way patterns are developed. It is, instead, an *A* among and between others, directly preceded and followed by *B*'s and, at one further remove, by *A*'s. The *A* here is not comparable to the *A* in pattern *BBBABBBA*, though it is the same letter. Given this theme, an actor can tell where he is only by calling up the future and the past. Theme, thus, generates a definition of current activity not by describing the immediate moment itself, but by describing the immediate moment's re-

---

[4] David Hays, *Personal Communication.*

lation to other moments. Theme is the past and future homology that informs the present.

Taking a common-sense situation as an example, we can see the application and violation of this rule in clinical descriptions of depersonalization. Depersonalization is clinically abnormal, sick, partly because the individual does not assume a determinate future, and thus cannot conceive the present as meaningful. If all acts are expected to lead to the same result, act A will be indistinguishable and hence, empty. To say that depersonalization is the impoverishment of imagination is to say that the present is meaningless because the future lacks design.

Elaboration. Once discovered, theme has its occasions. It is compounded and elaborated by locating its particulars over a series of chronologically discrete events. A theme cannot be said to exist unless it *appears,* unless it is portrayed, and it can only appear in the guise of individuated instances. In the guessing study described above, patterns did not immediately develop full-blown,—rather, there were a series of correct instances interrupted by a jumble of incorrect (discrete) ones. Incorrect tries were abandoned until, by trial and error, they were replaced by others that happened to be correct.

Suppose we are told before attending a political rally that an FBI man will be there, and we accept this as a theme to be documented. Because of this, our actions will take on a shape that they might not have, and in this sense the rally will contain a design. Furthermore, we would probably seek evidence to substantiate this theme by locating collateral occasions— for example, a stranger who by his dress (blue suit), ecology (always around the edges), and gaze (never on the rostrum), can be taken to be an FBI man. Here the FBI theme takes place through the items of its production.

Elaboration (blue suit, etc.) is the practical achievement of the identity of the interaction (FBI man) over its course, because it serves up collateral instances of that identity. When a particular of a theme is defined, something is immediately said about the particular and the theme, taken together, that overcomes the discreteness of chronological time. The particular, which is no more than a future possiblity as the theme develops, represents on the occasion of its presence the past-ness and future-ness of theme. What would be a mere happenstance without theme comes instead to be an exemplar. By the same token that theme, which would otherwise be vacant, is instantiated.

Fit. Instances do not always correspond neatly to theme or to one another. They also *test* the applicability of theme. Suppose the FBI man strikes up a conversation. Would we expect an attempt to discover our sympathies? What if he talked about baseball? In what way would this particular turn back and document, specify, or transform our original supposition of theme? As a sly but transparent effort by the FBI man to ingratiate himself? Or might we, assuming that baseball players behave at political rallies like FBI men, decide he is a baseball player instead, and thus call the original theme into question by leaving it without collateral? But this needn't be the end of it either. We could cease documenting the FBI theme through the behavior of others and turn instead to ourselves, considering very carefully what to do should the rally turn to matters ordinarily calling for our direct participation. Here we would be making room for the fact of the baseball player, while at the same time maintaining the possibility of the FBI man. Theme would continue to operate, although by very different occasions.

In the latter case, two instances interpreted as contradictory at one stage of the interaction were resolved as alternatives in their implications for theme, and thus compatible with one another. In everyday life, these occasions often take the form of excuses: Quality writers are permitted a "bad book," arguments over a painting are matters of "taste," psychotic offspring are chemical accidents, exceptions prove the rule. Phenotypic contradictions need not recommend genotypic transformations.

Authorship. There is a positive search for patterns, one that takes work and results in change. The vague relation between a sign and its social meaning has the consequence that the character of an object is not self-evident—the object does not unilaterally determine the meaning that comes to be assigned to it. If meaning were self-evident, "misunderstanding"[5] could never occur, because the character of the object and thus its treatment would be immanent and always correct. In this case, the idea of meaning would be redundant to reality. The sociological emphasis on feedback results from the realization that the social meaning of an object may have to be revised, that a definition at one point in time may undergo considerable revision at another. ("I thought it was love, but was it lust?")

---

[5] Gustav Ichheiser, "Misunderstandings in Human Relations," *American Journal of Sociology,* Part 2 (September, 1949), remains the best general description of this.

In accord with our intent to describe the definition of the situation, we need to see how the actor participates in definition even if this participation could be said, in another context, to be caused by his biography, his role, or the social structure. It must be possible for him to participate actively, in the sense that he is *doing* definition, that he is *engaged*, even when the outcome is determined by history: "The fish just might not be biting. But even if they are, the angler must still cast his line. It is a mistake, as Wittgenstein once pointed out, to think that if only nothing keeps me from walking, I shall walk."[6] After all, although the actor observes, he is not solely an observer. He is searching out a definition. Let us assume that a lover is uncertain as to whether the state of his affair is love or lust. Imagine how active would be the procedure of uncertainty: probably stalling behavior, which would be such as to firmly commit oneself to neither love nor lust, and yet so formulated as behavior to be seen by the other as either. Whereas actors presume to agree, they nevertheless *author* the particulars of the agreement—their definitions must be described in the active voice.

Revelation.   Some referents incapable of standing alone can be understood only in terms of some other social meaning, that is, they are syncategorematic. For example, " 'A mere child' is not something that is mere and a child."[7] Neither mere nor child can be used alone and preserve the meaning of the two taken together. Similarly, actors conceive some signs as being understandable only in terms of some immediately preceding or following referent and no other. These often take the form of "insights," wait-and-see's, and jokes. Moliere's gentleman is understandable to us, and to himself, only upon the discovery that he is prosy. Shaggy dog stories imply the imminence of a revelation that never comes. According to Bergson: "Many a comic form, that cannot be explained by itself, can indeed only be understood from its resemblance to another, which only makes us laugh by reason of its relationship with a third, and so on indefinitely."[8] Revelation in our case is evident in the reduction of surprise, as when one event connects with another in such a way as to make the first intelligible; and in the creation of surprise, as when events are

---

6 D. S. Shwayder, *The Stratification of Behavior* (New York: Humanities Press, 1965), p. 154.

7 W. V. O. Quine, *Word and Object* (Cambridge: M.I.T. Press, 1960), p. 103.

8 Henri Bergson, *Laughter, an Essay on the Meaning of the Comic,* Cloudesey Brereton, ed. (New York: The MacMillan Co., 1911) p. 65.

only juxtaposed, as it were, and call forth a transformation of the original understanding. It is the first which is usually said to be an insight, and the second which makes for comedy and worse. Both are discoveries from attention. In the search for meaning, some referents are discovered by syncategorematic connection to some other following or preceding referent.

It might be said that these features of emergence, which are supposed to represent social time, are nevertheless chronologically ordered as matters of fact. This is true, but necessary and not fatal. It is necessary in order to observe emergence empirically, and not fatal because these observations are conceptualized so as to be faithful to the social rather than chronological character of emergence.

With regard to observation, our concrete purchase on emergence must display the defined meaning of an event at one point before it could be noted empirically that such meaning has changed at another point. Hume can help us here.

It appears that, in single instances of the operations of bodies we never can, by our utmost scrutiny, discover anything but one event following another. . . . So that, upon the whole, there appears not, throughout all nature, any one instance of connexion, which is conceivable by us. All events seem entirely loose and separate. One event follows another; but we never can observe any tye between them. They seem *conjoined*, but never connected.[9]

It is fair to say that Hume, an empiricist in the technical philosophical sense who wrote during a time that required a polemic against the *a priori*, was both claiming the necessity of sense-data and setting its limits when he asserted that events seem conjoined, but never connected. (This is not quite correct either. Sense-data would not even seem conjoined unless the observer had an idea they might be.) When we restrict ourselves to observations, the observations themselves do not provide a linking account. Events are connected by conceptualization, not observation.

My theory represents an attempt to explain and understand what it is to *see* certain things *in* the movements of animate creatures. What we thus see and report upon might be styled as a kind of epiphenomenon with respect to animal movements and situational elements. They are phenomena which we see as residing in the movements only because we

---

[9] David Hume, *An Enquiry Concerning Human Understanding* (Oxford: The Clarendon Press, 1903), Section VII, Part II.

have these ways of thinking about the movements. You can, if you need a name, categorize my account as *conceptual epiphenomenalism.*[10]

The "tye" between our events, thus, is empirically chronological and conceptually social, a family of chronological cases connected by our emergent conceptualization of them. Given the general observational demands for establishing chronological matters of fact, on the one hand, and our conceptual thinking about social time, on the other, we have little to do but to observe discrete definitions according to the clock, and then to consider whether they form a concrescence of emergent time. This will enable us to observe definitional contrasts in some concrete setting which can be used to support or refute the overarching temporal conceptualization of emergence.

Relativity

This feature begins with the idea of the interchangeability of standpoints—what role theorists have called taking the role of the other. It has been said that role-taking is engaging in "as if" behavior, where the actor puts himself in the position of the other, and then rehearses his actions as if he were in fact the other.

Most of this work, however, has been devoted to such factors as empathic ability, skill in predicting what another will do, and the various conditions of self that influence these factors. Such work subsumes the very process we want to describe, namely, how we can even conceive the *possibility* of the practices through which empathy or skill can operate. Insofar as we can consider empathy with regard to role-taking (it would more properly be called self-taking), it is an "effect," because it analytically follows role-taking—it is really a role taken. Skill, oppositely, is a precondition of role-taking, because it precedes it. Skill is there before one faces the looking-glass, empathy only after one has looked into it. Empathy, skill, and the like are thus the expressions of some property that still has to be described—the *connection* between looking in and looking back. Our extrapolation of relativity must include the details of this phenomenon.

Earlier, it was suggested that, whereas relativity in its strictest sense does not literally allow complete and thoroughgoing perspectives to be

---

[10] Shwayder, *The Stratification of Behavior,* p. 13.

taken over by others, persons nevertheless can modify fragmentation by agreeing with one another that they are perceiving, believing, acting toward the same things, and, if their positions were reversed, would still be seeing the same things as the other person now does.

We can here turn to an adaptation of what Garfinkel calls the conditions of "perceived normality."[11] (He has them depict the way in which persons make all activities of others sensible, and so uses them more broadly than we will. They will be used here only as properties to be satisfied if role-taking is to occur, thereby overcoming the strictures of relativity.) We shall use them to observe how persons classify the environment and in so doing are enabled to decide that specific standpoints are interchangeable, as role-taking components of the definition of the situation.

It should be noted first that these components depend for their operation upon the relevance that the actor, not the sociologist, draws. They are social rather than sociological classifications, because they are proposed as devices used by common-sense actors for assessing the behavior of others, so they need not be mutually exclusive or logically coherent in and of themselves. Instead, once attributed by the actor, the sociologist must relate their use, account for the assessments by which persons and actions are placed within them, and so on, according to his own method and logic. Simply put, these components are treated as data.

Typicality. When a member interacts with another, he infers whether or not the other's behavior is representative of some group or category membership. He refers the particular behavior, as an instance, to a class of behaviors which to him is in some way comparable. Others are made into samples. When sociologists say fathers are role models for their sons, they are suggesting that sons classify the formulated behaviors as typically relevant to themselves and other males on the level of interaction.

---

[11] Garfinkel, "Common Sense Knowledge of Social Structures," N. J. M. Scher, ed., *Theories of the Mind* (New York: Free Press, 1962). The conditions reported here are an adaptation in the sense that some are invented by this writer, others of Garfinkel's are omitted, and those which are included are faithful to his purposes only in part. The reader may be interested in related classifications developed by Burke, Duncan, Brunswick, and Schutz. See Kenneth Burke, *A Rhetoric of Motives* (New York: Prentice Hall, 1950), p. 10 ff. and *passim;* Duncan, *Communication and the Social Order*, pp. 433-436; Egon Brunswick, "The Causal Texture of the Environment" and "Organismic Achievement and Environmental Probability," *Psychological Review*, 50 (1943), pp. 255-272; Schutz, *The Problem of Social Reality*, pp. 15-19 and *passim*, especially where he discusses typification.

Similarly, in regard to our earlier example, Jews who become medical doctors are often depicted as greedy because of their ethnic membership.

Likelihood. Members assess the probability of behavior, just as they do its typicality. This is the common-sense version of statistical curves, in that they can cast behavior as probable or improbable. Likelihood differs from typicality in that the actor, whereas he can predict a certain behavior as quite likely, may also characterize it as atypical. When a man cries, for example, one might be able to predict it, as in bereavement or drunkenness, although crying is not typical of men (socially). Further, actors often stop treating others as instances and instead orient toward them as special persons and not as representatives of types, as in the distinction between universalism and particularism, and in so doing predict what is likely in regard to the particular other. A bigot can treat particular ethnics independently of their group affiliations.

Causal texture. Members point to some phenomena as the conditions under which still other things will occur. The causal texture when a man cries, for example, may include drunkenness or bereavement. Causal texture is the common-sense version of cause and effect, the scenic auspices of events.

Technical efficiency. Members assert that some means are more efficient than others in achieving desired ends. They characterize behavior as appropriate or inappropriate, depending upon how it facilitates an objective.

Moral requiredness. Members assert the ontological necessity of some behavior independent of personal circumstance or desire. In the literature, these are usually referred to as values. Here, anything morally required is a prerequisite to bona fide membership in the interaction, so that its absence will result in exclusion.

Substantive congruency. Members determine whether others' substantive assessments of their environments are empirically right or wrong. "Empirically right or wrong" refers to accuracy of judgment rather than moral or normative correctness, so that etiquette or values would not be included in this category. If two persons argued about the principle of giving up one's seat to a lady, substantive congruency would not be the issue. However, if there were agreement on the principle but argument about whether or not another was a lady, substantive congruency would be the issue.

Actors can assess any single behavior in terms of all, a few, or just one of these components of relativity. Further, the outcome of assessment needn't be either positive or negative across all components, but could be positive for one and negative for another, as when crying is atypical but likely. Different components can also conflict, for example, the moral commandment that one shouldn't kill, even if it would be technically efficient in getting rid of a nagging wife.

Role-taking fails when interactants agree on none of these components. As actors fail to interchange standpoints, they will fail to communicate and become incapable of entering into the concerted actions that are characteristic of social order. When rules of use are inoperable, the world of probability with regard to expectations recedes behind the world of possibility, because the absence of rules would necessarily be accompanied by the absence of a delimited set of meanings. Under these circumstances, anything could be conceived to occur, nothing being differentiable from anything else; nothing being differentiable from anything else, all things would be equipossible; everything being equipossible, fiat would become impossible. The texture of the world would be completely open, no one inference being more capable of verification than any other. There could be no such thing as roles, subsuming reciprocal expectations, or the interdependent behavior that arises out of those expectations. Social life would have no systematic character, and could hardly be called social anymore.

In summary, there are potential specifications for each of our two major ideas: For emergence, the documentary method; and for relativity, the elements of "perceived normality." They provide a more detailed set of testable ideas and, if they are fruitful, should put teeth into conceptual and empirical ambiguities that mark theories of symbolic interaction, role, and social organization.

To decide whether the suggested components of the definition of the situation are, in fact, necessary for social order, we need first to construct a theoretical description of social disorder. This will enable us to contrast non-order with order, and to observe the presence or absence of emergence and relativity in each state.

V

Social Disorder

I have tried to describe what the definition of the situation could look like in an ongoing social interaction—to depict the organized construction of meaning by parties to a social relationship. Now it is necessary to move toward a test of those ideas, a test in two senses of the term. Most obviously, we must develop conditions in which we can observe emergence and relativity, and whether or not they turn out to be accurate delineations of what they are supposed to describe. This is the familiar sense of test in which the observer constructs some concrete set of activities within which his ideas can be expected to take empirical shape.

Less familiar, but equally important, we want to illuminate not just the sheer observability of the ideas, but also whether those ideas are important in a causal way, that is, whether, having been observed, they can also be said to have special consequence for the conceptual matters that they were meant to illuminate. It is this second task that we must address here, because it is of broader import and will set limits upon the kinds of direct observations that will serve the first.

We started by stating the problem of social order as an important sociological perspective. The definition of the situation was depicted as one aspect of that perspective. To be consistent with this statement of the problem of order, our test of the importance of the definition of the situation should provide an orderly and a disorderly scene, on the assumption that the contrast between the two will tell us just how important our version of defining the situation is. Implicit in any description of order is a description of disorder. If we can make disorder explicit in this particular case, we will serve a theoretical interest in the importance of our basic ideas as well as an empirical interest in a scene where the idea might take

observable form. To decide whether emergence and relativity are important to order, we must first construct a description of social disorder. In
sociology, disorder is anomie.

The history of the idea of anomie coincides with the history of the
problem of order, for anomie is the antithesis of order. Although the
particular noun was coined by Durkheim, Hobbes was discussing the
same thing when he talked of the war of each against all: Anomie, a norm-
less state, would make life solitary most of the time and brutish the rest.
Our concern with anomie is to discover the antithesis of our previous description of the elements of order—relativity, emergence, and the definition of the situation—and how it affects social interaction. Anomie will be
treated as a characteristic of the relation between the parties to an interaction insofar as they create and designate that relationship. That is, we
shall take the actor's version of the affair as a (potentially) anomic datum.
The actors, by their own actions in the experimental situation, will depict
the meaning of their activities, which will serve as the basis for our decision about their relationship. Just as we permit them to designate the
order of their situation, so shall we permit them to designate the disorder
of their situation.

Perhaps it would now be best to clarify what has only been implicit
up to this point. The definition of the situation is the sociological notion
analogous to the more general one of "meaning." An object is nothing, of
course, until it has meaning and thus can be differentiated in some way,
treated in some way, can provoke a response, can serve to indicate something else, and so forth. The difficulties in discussing meaning were briefly
mentioned in Chapter I with regard to the principle of variable meaning.
One need only review the many works on the topic in philosophy, literature, and the social sciences for evidence. I want to avoid reviewing these
arguments except to say that the position taken here is the one adopted by
Wittgenstein and others: Meaning is not what is referenced, but the rule
of use for a reference statement. That is, meaning is not the content of an
object description, but the rule by which that content comes to be assigned
in the first place (for us, emergence and relativity).

Consequently, the idea of anomie will only secondarily be discussed
as a "powerless feeling" or "felt need to innovate," for these are substantive descriptions of situations (objects) and can only follow upon the
failure of some prior rules of use—for example, the supposition that one
is capable of exerting influence. Anomie will be conceived as the
inapplicability of two kinds of rules used by actors in creating their

milieux. First, whatever the content of an interaction, the actor invokes the rule that it have intelligible purposes; second, whatever the content and intelligibility of purpose, the actor invokes the rule that there be some means by which purposes can be attained. The disorder of an interaction, then, hinges on a decision by the actor that one or the other of these rules is inoperative—that purpose is unintelligible or means unavailable.

This idea is very closely connected to the still unexplicated notion of "shared" norms, of a culture held in common. It is a notion we regularly invoke in comparing order with disorder (unshared norms). It has always been difficult to explain the statement that norms are shared. Shared norms and common culture go hand in hand, but just what we could expect these ideas to bring empirically, in the way of distinguishing various kinds of observable behaviors, is hard to realize. We read in introductory texts, for example, that norms are shared, and are then given the idea of subculture (read unshared). The social pie is sliced up by specialties and shored up by universals (or norms and values, roles and collectivities, sammy snicks and mickey mudds).

Now the analytic and empirical inadequacy of leaving universals and specialties at that becomes apparent if we think of them as nothing but content, as in a game: Moving forward two spaces, backward three, jumping over another object on the board, and so on. This description doesn't recommend anything (Is it chess or checkers?) because we are without the rules by which the moves become sensible. The pristine stranger, for example, can observe life around him, but it makes little sense to do so because he is without the rules of use that are common to those engaged in that life. Unless he quickly learns the purposes and means, we could say that his relations are anomic.

For both the gamer and the stranger, it is not the moves themselves that can be depicted as universals or specialties, but rather the *rules of use* by which they are described and enforced in the game or culture. To point to a telephone and say it is black is not merely to say a telephone is black, but to use a rule by which something can be called the color black.[1]

With regard to anomie, it is not that things are "no good" or whatever a subject might say when he is in that state; that is merely an outcome of some disjuncture in rules of use. Rather, anomie is a characteristic of a relationship that *prevents certain rules from being applied*, namely, the

---

[1] I have here blurred the distinction between rules for characterizing an object (color) and for using it (to talk).

two common culture-making rules comprising the intelligibility of purpose and the availability of means for attaining that purpose. In the color example, anomie would be present when a subject is unable to decide that describing the color of the telephone is the purpose of the activity, or that there is any other apparent purpose; or when he is unable to construct some means to describe the telephone. Whatever the content of the interaction, whatever in particular is designated as "the situation" by the subject, the interaction will be considered a disorderly one when we can observe in his behavior that one or both of these rules are no longer applicable. Anomie exists, in our case, when the actor finds that the rules for depicting the activity are inapplicable.

It might be said that such a definition of disorder allows for "mistake" to be called orderly, that is, the use of a rule by one party when another party (the observer, or some other interactant) would consider it inapplicable. This is true, but it should bring no objection unless we want to return to the imposed standard exemplified by "false consciousness." We shall here treat anomie as something that must be experienced by actors, whether or not it is a result of some mistake. Because we are dealing with men as meaning-makers, disorder must be experienced before it can be said to occur in the definition of the situation.

Just as we earlier specified the way emergence and relativity look to the actors involved, so must we now specify how actors will express the inapplicability of these two rules. We shall do so by incorporating three kinds of actors' expressions as anomie—meaninglessness, powerlessness, and innovation. These will serve as substantive descriptions arrived at by invoking the purpose and means rules. Disorder, then, is not essentially a description of powerlessness, meaninglessness, or innovation; rather, it is the reporting of them as a description of the inapplicability of the two rules. They indicate the shared or unshared character of the relation. Thus, anomie for us reflects the removal of conditions by which actors presume a shared and therefore common culture.

By powerlessness is meant the actor's assertion that his own behavior is instrumentally unrelated to the purpose he seeks. Whereas the actor may be clear about purpose, powerlessness is his assertion that, whatever he does, the purpose will not be brought nearer to consummation. The actor states that his environment is unresponsive and his actions ineffectual.

During innovation, means are available, but the actor presumes that they are inappropriate from the point of view of those with whom he interacts. The mark of innovation is not the absence of a channel toward purpose, but the lack of acceptability by others. The environment is only deviously responsive to the actor's actions.

Whereas innovation and powerlessness are concerned with unavailable means, meaninglessness is a characteristic of unintelligible purpose. The latter precludes understanding, because purpose is analytically prior to the delineation of possible means. The interaction is not sensible to the actor, for what can be a means to no purpose? ("Ritualism," the transformation of a means to an end, is, of course, purposeful activity *from the point of view of the actor,* however it might be described by others.) Meaninglessness is a state in which phenomena lack clarity and are, therefore, incapable of description.

Now what general kinds of interaction can be inferred from these expressions of anomie? What can actions that are powerless, meaningless, or innovative imply in the way of the conditions that bring them about? Most obviously and generally, they can imply either a changed or disintegrated social order. That is, the concrete responses of persons to the environment can reflect or be determined by the absence of the conditions of order or a change in the substance of that order. We must allow for the possibility that increments to the original order, as process, can momentarily disrupt interaction, not so perniciously as to destroy it, but modestly enough to change its direction. An interaction may halt for a while, then pick up again in a novel direction, in a series of stable behaviors interrupted by intermittent anomie. Allowing for this possibility enables us to observe re-starting mechanisms so that we may gain more information about order's temporary or permanent failure, and, conversely, temporary and terminal anomie.

Suppose, for example, that a rich and confident Phi Beta Kappa asks his advisor whether he should continue on to graduate school, and the advisor answers "no." Suppose, too, that the student is surprised (shocked?) by this, so that he finds the interaction with his advisor unintelligible. Will the interaction halt forever? Or will he reconstruct the scene and, in so doing, find that the advisor has mistaken him for someone else, is an adherent of restrictive admission to the occupation, or some other notion. Such a reconstruction will permit him to sensibly complete the interview, albeit with a very different set of definitions than those with which he began. We are asking here if anomie is an absolute point of no return for the relationship, a point which cannot be proceeded from, because there is no place left to go; or if there are socially navigable alternatives that replace the original course and permit agreement between parties that the substance of their relationship has changed but not disappeared.

A difficulty in this procedure is the establishment of a point beyond which we are no longer interested, because the action, while shifting, would be far removed from either permanent or temporary anomie. Suppose the Phi Beta Kappa was not so sure of the answer he would get. In this case the answer contains new information, but is it a surprise or merely an ordinary addition to the student's stock of knowledge about his advisor? We must decide where to draw the line between temporary failure and the constant shifts that are minor and continuous, but not related to anomie in any direct way. There is no good theoretical reason for establishing cutting points here or there, because anomie as a process is so vague and indeterminate that there are no valid *a priori* distinctions; the reason for allowing for temporary failure in the first place is to find out more about it. Therefore, we will wait and establish cutting points empirically and let the interaction itself tell us if there is such a thing as temporary failure, and how it can be distinguished from both permanent failure and the ordinary changes which do not at all threaten the continuity of interaction.

We should point out again that the intention of the preceding discussion of anomie is to give us some information about order and the definition of the situation, for a study of some phenomenon can be enhanced by inspecting its opposite. What better way to find the conditions of definition than to program a situation (anomie) where it may not be present? This is simply an observational version of Weber's mental experiment, in which he suggests thinking away the element under study and then thinking in the consequence of its absence. The difference in our approach is that removal will be empirical rather than imagined.

Summary

If theorizing entails providing conceptual solutions to empirical questions, and if we refuse the theorist exclusive rights to his ideas, we can summarize much of sociology as offering answers to the problem of order.

Beginning with Hobbes, many have not taken orderly interpersonal relations for granted. They have undertaken the large task of searching for principles of order. Starting from the ground up proffers a technical advantage because we can observe behaviors that occur in face-to-face interaction rather than in the gigantic arenas of institutions. It is easier to control the interactions of a few concrete individuals than the behavior of governments and economies.

Whereas *Mind, Self and Society* is Mead's best-known work, he has more directly approached the social order of interaction in other writings, especially when he describes relativity and emergence as the ways persons overcome the temporal and spatial boundaries that distinguish them from one another. Logically, these boundaries should lead one to believe there can be no order, but it is a logic challenged by our everyday observations.

Emergence makes disparate slices of time continuous enough in their meaning to maintain concerted activity, whereas relativity makes disparate segments of space contiguous enough to allow communication from body to body. These ideas are main elements in the solution of our problem, but they are neither entirely clear nor specific, so we have had to include other ideas to complete the solution. Elaboration of the documentary method of interpretation can fashion the workings of emergence, the connection of past, present, and future; perceived normality can detail relativity, the connection of meaning across space. *Emergence and the documentary method, on one hand, and relativity and perceived normality, on the other, can be conceived as answers to any question asking how definitions are orderly enough to make interaction more than random.*

Once beyond these ideas, however, we are left with the empirical dilemma that faces anyone who questions the obvious: How do we program its antithesis? We want to conceptualize and observe a nonorder because it enables us to study order. By taking order out, by placing it in jeopardy, we can test the importance of the basic ideas. Fortunately, anomie can be construed as the randomization of orderly definition. To the extent that there are no common meanings, no communication, no norms, we have Hobbes' war of all against all. Once we reduce anomie to the intelligibility of purpose and availability of means, we can study the interactions that produce, modify, and eliminate it, and, in so doing, test the organizing power of emergence and relativity.

The conceptual bones of this investigation, therefore, are (1) emergence and relativity as specifications of the definition of the situation and prerequisite to social interaction; and (2) anomie, as the change, or dissolution, of the definition of the situation.

VI

Method
and Design

Methods, being theories of data, tell us how to link concepts and observations, whereas designs carry through and do the actual linking in particular studies. So that the reader may know how this analysis comes out the way it does, and be able to decide how it might have turned out differently, I shall put the design in context by describing the stage and subject matter of this investigation, some general methodological requirements for any test of the definition of the situation, along with more specific ones for emergence and relativity, and the actual procedures and form of analysis used here to meet those requirements.

This is a study in which detailed laboratory controls and statistical tests have been purposely avoided. Because this kind of work is often treated as a last resort for those who, talented perhaps in sensate cognition, lack a capacity for arithmetic, I shall discuss why it is necessary in appropriate places.

Stage

It is now established that no single method is appropriate to every proposition. Inquiry begins with a problem; there are different kinds of problems; hence there must be different methods. One way of distinguishing a problem, and, therefore, methods, is the problem's stage of development, beginning with Dewey's "originating question" and proceeding to finite replications of detailed hypotheses. An indeterminate problem, where one has little more than speculation for hypotheses, is quite different from a replication, where one has true theory, hypotheses, data, and analysis already in view. In the former, we must ascertain just what "facts" are relevant to the problem in order to formulate it more precisely; in a replication these facts are expressly set out for observation. The definition of the situation is often invoked but seldom specified.

> The social act is seen as a continuous process of defining the situation, with each definition evolving, in large part, out of antecedent definitions. In effect, the act becomes a series of contingencies. Once a choice has been made, there may be a commitment to it which will determine most of the steps in a future course of action.[1]

A "choice" is here used synonymously with definition and made the determinant of a social act or process, then of succeeding acts, processes, and definitions, because it "commits" the actor to a future course. But there is nothing to indicate how a choice is made as the critical determinant of commitment, except other choices preceding other commitments, which is of course circular. How *are* choices made, and what determines an evolving, that is, elaborated, set of choices or definitions? (I have ignored the indefinite conditionals "may" and "must" in the above statement for the sake of clarity. It is the unspecified meaning of choice that makes it necessary for their author to use these terms without stipulation.)

Another commentary might be suggested in answer to the query posed of the first.

> The choice of definitions depends upon one's sentiments toward the significant others who serve as representatives of reference groups ... (and) ... the reference group is that group whose presumed perspective is used by the actor as the frame of reference.[2]

It would be vacuous to proffer this answer, however. In this instance choice of definition becomes dependent upon sentiment toward significant others, so we are left with the same difficulty in a different language: How do sentiments operate in the act of definition? They may move the actor toward adopting a perspective, but how is the perspective finally adopted,

---

[1] Rose, "Introductory Comment," in Arnold Rose, ed., *Human Behavior and Social Process*, p. 321.

[2] Tamotsu Shibutani, "Reference Groups and Social Control," in Arnold Rose, ed., *Human Behavior and Social Process*, pp. 141, 132.

once the actor is moved? We must ask this unless we want to assume that
definition is automatic, immanent, and totally self-generating, a very unlikely possibility if we take surprise, misunderstanding, and the like as an
indication of disjuncture between what sentiment leads us to expect as
against the activity being defined. Finally, the definition of the situation:

Refers to the individual's prior conception of and attitude toward a
given situation that influence his behavior when he meets that situation.[3]

The term "prior" here suggests that nothing much happens in the
situation itself. "Conception" as opposed to "attitude" implies a more
objectified version of what the situation will be, whereas attitude expresses
a corresponding affect about it. "When he meets the situation" indicates
he comes to know he is in it rather automatically, rather than having to
decide he is in it, and that his prior attitudes and conceptions, his predispositions, are mechanically triggered into play.

If we think of individuals encountering one situation after another,
the utility of "prior" fades, because in no situation would conceptions
and attitudes change or become problematic except in previous ones. This
would lead to gorgeous reductionism.

Even granting that Huntington's formulation is dimly accurate, we
still want to know how attitudes and conceptions are enacted once the
situation arises, so that we might reduce the ambiguity of the term "influence." How does one define a situation contemporaneously, as he meets
it? How is coping with situations action? Since the purposes of the quoted
authors are to depict other processes by invoking the definition of the
situation, their descriptions may not be inadequate. But they do exemplify
how the definition of the situation is usually reduced (without a set of
rules for reduction, and, therefore, only likened) to reference groups,
perspectives, culture, or significant others, without explaining precisely
how the actor adopts the standards of the reference group or how the
reference group standards are transferred to the actor, how a significant
other influences him except as a model, or how culture enters the situation
except by invoking sentiment, aspiration, or socialization. These reduc-
tions rely on attraction (or avoidance) but fail to specify the link between attraction and definition. The idea of defining the situation, so often

---

[3] Mary Jean Huntington, "The Development of a Professional Self Image," in
Merton, Reader, and Kendall, eds., *The Student Physician*, p. 183n.

a bulwark for other inferences, has not itself received very great consideration.

Moving closer to the problem at hand, the components of emergence and relativity have never been put together as dimensions of the definition of the situation. It follows that the design should be flexible enough to see if they operate at all, to see how they operate together, and to produce behavior we have overlooked. We will have been methodologically successful if we can engender these kinds of observations and so push the definition of the situation toward greater specification.

Subject Matter

"Public definitions of a situation (prophecies or predictions) become an integral part of the situation and thus affect subsequent developments. This is peculiar to human affairs. Predictions of the return of Halley's comet do not influence its orbit."[4] This investigation must permit the distinctly prophetic (and reconstructing) capacity to be observed, because the definition of the situation is the incorporation of that capacity into a social setting. However, this very characteristic makes the definition of the situation an ephemeral aspect of social interaction, because meaning is seldom self-evident unless it is also, for the social scientist at least, trivial. The definition of the situation is not in one-to-one correspondence with the material trappings of attributes such as age, marital record, or having long hair, but rather symbolically contains these attributes in a number of ways. Census data, for example, tell us nothing about the definitional processes they signify until the population's normative and institutional structure is brought to bear upon them.

On top of this basic difficulty, which is intrinsic to symbolic behavior, there is the tendency for those in the system to take definitions for granted. Questions like "How do you decide he is untrustworthy?" "Why do you love your children?" or "What do you mean, you had a good time?" often choke up otherwise articulate respondents. As a matter of fact, the sociologist's technical interview paraphernalia of probe, contingent ques-

---

[4] Merton, *Social Theory and Social Structure*, p. 423.

tion, and the like, have been developed, in part, to overcome the presumption to agreement that obscures definitional matters. In Durkheim's terms, definitional matters are saturated with the unstated rules of contract.[5]

Consequently, the definition of the situation is difficult to observe, without leaping inference, when subjects talk about everyday matters in an everyday manner. Nor can it be directly observed in such social processes as aging, getting married, or growing long hair. Definition is so embedded in everyday interaction that we must design a test that uses laboratory procedures to unwrap it. By eliminating the round of *en vivo* activities that ordinarily obscure it, the definition of the situation can be cast in high relief for more direct observation. The laboratory also allows continuous observation of the entire interaction, which is especially advantageous here because we have not fixed the points at which emergence and relativity will develop and change.

Having decided that the laboratory is a fruitful place to study the definition of the situation in general, we may now address emergence and relativity as our particular conception of definition. We have already implied a two-fold design: (1) Observation of the activity of defining a situation, to see if emergence and relativity can be detected, and (2) observation of anomie, to see if emergence and relativity disappear. If emergence and relativity operate during the definition of the situation, they have descriptive validity. If they disappear during anomie, we can infer that, besides being merely a part of order, they are functionally salient to it. Social order and emergence and relativity would, in this case, be interdependent as well as coextensive. We shall therefore seek to discover if emergence and relativity are sensible descriptions of the definition of the situation by creating two test conditions, order and anomie, in which we expect two corresponding states of definition, the presence of emergence and relativity in the orderly condition, and the absence of emergence and relativity in the anomic condition. Our first step toward observation implies the following:

Order	**Anomie**
emergence and relativity present	emergence and relativity absent

---

[5] Durkheim, *On the Division of Labor in Society*, pp. 192 ff.

When we add the components of emergence, relativity, and anomie we will get the following (see pp. 69-75 for complete descriptions):

Order	Anomie
Emergence	Unintelligible purpose
theme	*meaninglessness*
elaboration	Unavailable means
fit	*powerlessness*
authorship	*innovation*
revelation	
Relativity	
typicality	
likelihood	
causal texture	
technical efficiency	
moral requiredness	
substantive congruency	

This arrangement generates observations that will illuminate the following general descriptive and causal possibilities:

1. If emergence and relativity operate during order (description): Can the subject be observed to invoke theme, authorship, typicality and the like as he goes about defining the situation? According to our criteria, does he make sense of the situation at all?

Furthermore, do any specific components of emergence and relativity operate more often than others, or in association with others, during order? Does the subject address theme, say, more often than typicality? Does he keep documenting some previously discovered pattern of meaning as he interacts, at the expense of assessing the group ties of those around him?

2. If emergence and relativity or their components fail to operate during anomie (necessity): Do we now observe the absence of theme, typicality, and all other components? Alternatively:

a. Which components of emergence or relativity operate more often than others, or in association with others, during anomie? If meaning is present, is the subject preoccupied with fitting surprising acts to the theme originally supplied? Is he bewildered and confused? What components does he invoke in these states?

b. Which components of emergence and relativity operate in association with particular expressions of anomie? Are powerlessness, innovation, and meaninglessness differentially sensible to the subject insofar as they are consistently defined in different ways? Does it regularly occur that meaninglessness, for example, is accompanied by causal texture statements such as "This experiment is terribly difficult, I can't see the other person or talk to him directly."?

3. If anomie or any of its components is immediately preceded by particular components of emergence and relativity (process, influence, necessity) : Does a search for the moral status of things usually precede meaninglessness? Do subjects say something like "This is a terrible idea, no one should ever kill," just before becoming totally bewildered with regard to the purposes of their situation?

4. If anomie or any of its components is a permanent or temporary condition (description) : Once bewildered, do subjects remain bewildered? Or is total silence, for example, followed by a re-discovery of themes, by elaborating them, and, in general, by connecting the environment to purpose?

When temporary, which components of emergence and relativity reappear? If these components are different than those appearing in the original order and in anomie, we may infer that they are alternatives to them. If subjects do not remain bewildered, what are they doing with regard to emergence and relativity? The same things they did *before* anomie? Or different things? Does the defining emphasis shift, not only as between the original order and anomie, but also between the original order and the new order? Does a subject go from statements such as "I need money," to "I don't know what I need," to "I have everything I need," as the interaction moves from order to anomie to order?

The design is clearly both "qualitative" and "functional." It is qualitative because presence and absence are discrete design conditions that correspond to our conceptualization of emergence and relativity as noncontinuous. It is functional because we have suggested that emergence and relativity are requisites of orderly interaction. The introduction of anomie is meant to test this necessity. The tactic of removal, in which a discrete item is observed in one condition, then removed in another, providing a contrast between conditions which can be related to removal of the item, makes it possible to design a test that is both qualitative and functional. The greater the (presumed) functional importance of the item, the greater the likelihood of clear effects because of its removal. In our case, we remove emergence and relativity in order to study their necessity for orderly interaction.

It remains now to develop a laboratory test where the definition of the situation can be cast out from its everyday enclosure, and, in so doing, can engender data relevant to these relations. I shall describe such a test in detail, and then briefly discuss how it meets these requirements.[6]

Procedure

In order to hide the real purpose of the experiment, subjects are solicited for a study of psychotherapy. They are told that such therapy is presently a complicated and time-consuming method of giving advice about personal problems, and that the experimenter is looking for a simpler method. Upon arriving for the experiment, S is told to think over his problem, relate some background to it, and then ask questions about it that can be answered only yes or no. The experimenter, meanwhile, has gone to another room and gives his "answer" through an intercom, but his answer has been predecided by consulting a table of random numbers and would be the same regardless of the question asked. S then records what he "understands" the answerer to be telling him, what the yes or no means to him in terms of his problem. The answerer (experimenter) is unable to hear S's understanding of his answer because S shuts off the intercom except while he asks the question and gets the answer. This process continues through ten questions and answers, after which S is to summarize what he has learned from the whole conversation.

Thus, there is a beginning to the experiment, in which S's background statement indicates his original definition; a middle, in which this definition, as he comments on each answer, should be elaborated or modified; and an end, in which the final summary definition can be related back to the beginning and middle.

To create disruption and anomie, different subjects receive different proportions of yeses and noes, ranging from fifty-fifty splits to all yeses or all noes. This is to ensure discrepancy without having to tamper with the random character of the answers, and without having to rely upon the guesses of the experimenter. It is expected that(1) the greater the split, the more likely that disruption will occur, because S will be surprised by

---

[6] For another description of this procedure, see Harold Garfinkel, "Common Sense Knowledge of Social Structures," in Scher, ed., *Theories of the Mind*, pp. 20-28.

getting the same answer to so many questions; and (2) disruption will occur in those even splits when S asks the same question more than once and gets a different random answer the second time. Each of these techniques should make S entertain the possibility that the answers he gets are not motivated by the questions he asks. This in turn should make him question whether his original definition of the situation, psychotherapy, is actually occurring, and so create the possibility of anomie.

To control any psychological dispositions to anomie, each S is administered the Srole scale at the beginning of the session.[7] Under these circumstances, responses to order and disorder can be more surely attributed to the test conditions, should expected differences materialize during the course of the investigation.

Discussion of Procedure

The random-answer technique is a one-sided interaction, stemming almost entirely from S, so it corresponds to the stricture against both circumscribing and determining his construction of the definition. Because there is a one word response, or interaction, from E to S, the meanings assigned are largely a product of the subject's own work. Further insurance is obtained by removing the experimenter from sight, eliminating meanings which could be determined by his tone of voice or facial appearance. The experimenter, in effect a silent partner to the interaction, is a neutral stimulus, and does not *necessarily* determine meaning. Because E is designed to portray as few of the characteristics of others as possible and still have interaction, any interpretations over and above these few should bring emergence and relativity to the observable surface in S's recorded comments. By exaggerating the amount and location of work that goes into constructing a definition—by leaving it to S to deneutralize E, E's advice, and the experimental situation— we are assuming that S is manifestly engaged in the same forms of activity he uses in everyday life, but that he will be unable to use the standard patter that obscures the definition of the situation when conventional vehicles of interaction are present.

The creation of anomie, in which even this modicum of structure is eliminated, can in this procedure be accomplished in two ways: By con-

---

[7] Leo Srole, "Social Integration and Certain Corollaries: An Exploratory Study," *American Sociological Review*, 21 (1956), pp. 709-716.

tradicting answers given earlier in the experiment and by giving S disproportionate yeses or noes. Each of these gambits is likely to call the ostensible reason for the experiment into doubt, that reason being a search for a simple, less time-consuming method of psychotherapy. As S perceives contradictory responses, he may well wonder about the legitimacy of the experimenter or the experiment, or both. This should make the situation dubious in terms of his original understanding, that is, the original "order" of the experiment should undergo some disruption. The second, meant to create the same effect, should make S wonder if the answers are in fact motivated by the questions, because answers are all or nearly all the same. As he wonders about this, he should call the experiment into doubt, if he assumes psychotherapy requires replies that are intended to be answers to questions. Each of these conditions should disrupt the order by calling the situation and the experimenter into doubt.

Thus, a modicum of "other" should both make the process of definition manifest and, in conjunction with random answers, call even this modicum into question.

Design Corollaries
of the Conceptual Components
of Emergence, Relativity, and Anomie

Our next step is to relate the conceptual components of emergence and relativity to their corollaries in the question-answer design. Each corollary will be treated as an observable of each component in the sense that they are concrete test representations of concepts and can be used as a set of coding instructions. Each component of emergence, relativity, and anomie is listed along with its experimental parallel. To clarify both the distinct and related aspects of the two, I use an adaptation of Kaplan's "act meaning" and "action meaning" to refer to design corollaries and conceptual components, respectively. Act meaning refers to subject behavior in the experimetal procedure, action meaning to the transformation of act meaning into the perspective of the definition of the situation.[8] Included

---

[8] Abraham Kaplan, *The Conduct of Inquiry* (San Francisco: Chandler Publishing Co.), pp. 32-33. For Kaplan, "Act meaning" is the meaning of the act to the actor, and "Action meaning" the meaning of the same act to the social scientist. I am using the terms here in comparable but not synonymous ways, to refer to the meaning of behavior in the experimental setting and to its conceptual meaning, respectively.

are snatches of laboratory interactions that illustrate each corollary (protocols are examined more fully in a later chapter).

I

Conceptual Components (Action Meaning)	**Design Corollaries** (Act Meaning)

Theme

Actors assume that a pattern of meaning is to be discovered in the events they observe.

The subject assumes that an answer to his stated problem can be obtained, as indicated by the fact that he continues to ask substantive questions until either (1) resolution or (2) termination of the experiment. ("Do you think a bank loan is a wise course of action?")

Any question referring to the experimental situation rather than to the substance of the problem will indicate that the pattern is no longer in use, because the subject will be addressing some other issue rather than an answer to his problem. Nonsubstantive questions will be treated as a suspension of the assumption that an answer can be obtained at some point during the interaction. ("If your advice isn't worthwhile, am I wasting my time and yours discussing the problem?")

Elaboration

The discovered theme is compounded and elaborated throughout a series of discrete events,

Each succeeding comment, following each answer, should embellish and detail the problem, accommodating to each event insofar as is necessary to maintain the theme.

Fit

The signal relation between an event and the assumed underlying theme is vague enough so that events which call the theme into question will be resolved as alternative, rather than refutory, in their implications for the underlying theme.

whereas the summary should provide an end result of what the subject has learned during the interview. Whenever one comment qualifies, modifies, or expands the preceding comment, and whenever the summary differs from the background given at the beginning of the interview, elaboration is present. ("Not only should I stop writing to her, *I should not even talk to her friends.*")

When *S* perceives answers as giving different kinds of advice for the same problem, he will treat them, not as illegitimate, but as legitimate ones between which *he* must discover congruency.

Each subject has been recruited ostensibly to help study methods of psychotherapy. It can safely be assumed that he believes answers are directly motivated by the questions asked, rather than randomly given. Because answers are random, however, and because the subject can be expected to ask similar questions more than once in some cases, unclear and contradictory answers are possible. It is expected that the subject will manipulate the answers he conceives as contradictory or unclear so that he can maintain his definition of the situation (the underlying theme) by providing "reasons" for such answers which rid them of their contradiction. The subject's own description of the answer will be used to indicate contradiction, as well as any indication that an answer is surprising or unexpected. ("Hmm, you told me to apply before, and now you tell me not to go on to school after all. *Gee what am I to do with this? Hmm. Oh, I know. You know more about me now.* I should apply but not go on to school unless I change my study habits. Yes. Of course.")

Authorship

A positive search for thematic homologies occurs throughout variations in the environment.

The meanings of different answers to different questions are connected. *S* interprets one answer in terms of both previous answers and potential future answers and questions.

The "different environments" are the different questions put by *S*. Connection will occur when these different questions are related to his overarching problem. Different environments have been connected to the degree that each comment and summary incorporate materials that occur at some other point in the interview. Explicit reference to past or future questions and answers indicates authorship. ("You said liquor wasn't dangerous. Now pot isn't either. If I can find out about horse, we'll be able to decide whether or not I'll get caught.")

Revelation

When the actor observes an event, he assumes there is a referent, and the referent chosen is the one corresponding to formerly discovered homologous themes.

S is asked to comment upon what the answers mean, what the experimenter is saying when he responds yes or no. This attribution of meaning will be treated as an event observed by *S*. Revelation will occur when another meaning is attached to this specific attributed meaning. Any attribution of one meaning to an answer, followed by a statement indicating the meaning of the first attribution, will be coded as revelation. ("You mean I shouldn't write. I shouldn't write at all. Not only will it be harder on him, *he might even misunderstand.*")

II

Conceptual Components of Relativity
(Action Meaning)

Design Corollaries
(Act Meaning)

Typicality

When a person observes others, he is interested in whether or not others' behavior is representative of some referent group, category, or behavior. He treats behavior as an instance of a class of behaviors.

S treats both his own questions and *E*'s answers as instances of types of questions and answers. *S* states answers are instances of psychotherapy, psychologist's orientation, or of the experimental situation. ("Isn't that just like a psychiatrist?")

Likelihood

Persons assess the probability of the behaviors they observe.

S expects some answers and doesn't expect others. When *S* expects an answer even though he characterizes it as unusual, or when he doesn't expect an answer even though he characterizes it as usual, he is depicting the likelihood of the answer. ("That's what I thought . . . but no one else would.") ("Well, I don't know what to say about that . . . of course everyone else does it.")

Causal texture

Persons point to phenomena as the causal agents of other phenomena, as the conditions under which an event occurs.

S explicitly points to circumstances in the experiment as the reasons for the answers he gets, such as E's not knowing S, not being in the room with him, and the yes-no procedure. ("How can I make him understand? How can he make me understand? We never saw one another before, and we can't see one another now.")

Technical efficiency

Persons assess the instrumental efficacy of behavior in terms of a stated goal.

S assesses the efficiency of given answers, as well as the whole experiment, insofar as they help him to resolve his problem given in the background statement. ("My problem isn't being helped at all.")

Moral requiredness

Persons assert the ontological necessity of some behavior, a necessity they treat as independent of circumstances or the desires of themselves and others.

S assesses the propriety of answers independently of any of the other features of perceived normality. Whether the answer is likely, typical, causally textured, efficient, or congruent, it will also be characterized as morally right or wrong, for no reason other than rectitude. The other features of perceived normality, as well as the experimental situation, will be held irrelevant in his depiction of some answers. ("I don't care what's best, my father shouldn't leave my mother.")

Substantive congruency

Persons assess others' behavior in terms of its empirical accuracy, independently of moral judgments.

S will agree or disagree with the meaning he attributes to *E* when commenting upon his answers. After he has assessed the meaning of an answer, he will also assess its empirical accuracy, as in stating "he is correct," or "he is incorrect." ("Bull. I'll never get out of it that way.")

III

Conceptual Components of Anomie
(Action Meaning)

Design Corollaries
(Act Meaning)

Powerlessness

The expectation that one's own behavior cannot determine the outcome he seeks.

S states that his questions do not affect the kinds of answers he receives, even though he can attribute meaning to them. ("It doesn't matter what I think, he is going ahead with his advice.")

Meaninglessness

The inability to interpret environmental events, to apply norms to

S cannot impute any meaning to the answers he receives. Silence,

observations.

statements that "I don't know what to say," or "I don't understand," lack of any attribution to the test situation or S's problem, will all indicate meaninglessness. ("Oh, no. Oh.")(One minute silence.) ("Well. No, huh?")

Innovation

The expectation that socially unapproved behaviors are most efficacious in attaining desired outcomes.

S continues to comment upon answers, but states he is doing so only to finish the experiment. He no longer makes an effort to impute meanings so much as to complete the task. ("I don't care what he's up to. I'll just go along and ask the same question over again. Who cares?")

Whereas the procedures described so far will permit observation of order and anomie, we have yet to insure a true test by making it falsifiable. It should not, of course, be inevitable that order display emergence and relativity and anomie display nothing. In the interest of falsifiability, we must specify some *condition indicators*, empirically independent of emergence and relativity, to signal that the interaction is, in fact, in a certain state (order, disruption, anomie), and which require that emergence and relativity ensue or not, as the case may be. The orderly condition will be considered to have occurred when S follows instructions and discusses the content of his problem. Disruption will be considered to have occurred when S says an answer is contradictory, addresses the split between yeses and noes, or entertains the possibility that the ostensible purpose (psychotherapy) is not the actual purpose. Anomie will be considered to have occurred when S *withdraws* the ostensible purpose, whether or not he substitutes another. Following this, protocols will be analyzed for components of emergence and relativity, on the one hand, and anomie on the other. We will have been right to the degree that emergence and relativity appear and disappear as expected.

Our final programmatic task is to give a running account of conceptual components, design corollaries, and condition indicators, in order to embrace the whole design as a test of courses of interaction and definition:

PHASE 1: *Order.* Subject gives background to the problem, asks questions, and applies meaning to answers by commenting on them. Emergence and relativity operate. Condition indicator: Subject follows instructions and is exclusively concerned with the content of his problem.

PHASE 2: *Disruption.* Subject construes answers as contradictory or disproportionate. Constructed definition of the situation is challenged, suspension of order while challenge is resolved toward order or anomie. Emergence and relativity expected to shift in emphasis. Condition indicators: Subject states contradiction, addresses split, or entertains possibility that ostensible purpose (psychotherapy) is not actual purpose.

PHASE 3: *Order.* Subject resolves disruption in favor of original definition. Condition indicators: Subject reinvokes ostensible purpose or states answers not contradictory. Components of emergence and relativity in Phases 2 and 3 that are different from those in Phase 1 will be considered functional alternatives to those in Phase 1.

OR

PHASE 3a: *Anomie.* Powerlessness, meaninglessness, innovation occur; emergence and relativity disappear. Condition indicator: Subject *withdraws* ostensible purpose, may or may not substitute another purpose. If anomie is a terminal state, interaction should cease. Condition indicators: Subject sits without talking or asking questions or tells the experimenter he is finished before he has asked ten questions, received ten answers, or summarized the conversation.

PHASE 4: *Reorder.* If anomie is a temporary state, emergence and relativity reappear. Condition indicator: Subject reinstates ostensible purpose. Any difference in emergence and relativity from Phases 1, 2, and/or 3 is a consequence of, or functional alternative to, anomie.

Units of analysis are background, each question, the commentary for each answer, and summary. They are natural ones in the sense that they are demarcated by the laboratory procedure and the instructions given *S*. In accord with conceptualization, a single unit can exhibit any number of components. Units for the appearance of theme are the questions the subject asks throughout the interview. Units for all other components of emergence and relativity are the subject's comments following each answer and the final summary. Any comment or summary can contain every component, only a few, or none. (As will be seen shortly, comments are usually about a paragraph long; therefore, most of these passages display more than a single component.)

Each interview, fully recorded on tape, is analyzed in this manner. It differs from the typical content analysis in that data are engendered by and for the analyst, and by the fact that we are not counting words. What we shall take as a raw datum is not an already interpreted version of some event, reconstituted by another observer, with another purpose, for another audience. It is simply a recording of vocal behavior (including silence). It is a more complete record than, say, a survey, because the subject's behavior comes to the coder without having been filtered through the written interpretations of an interviewer (this two-step survey flow holds even when the roles of coder and interviewer reside in the same person, of course).

There are drawbacks to the procedure, but they are not critical. First, the experimental situation makes it impossible to observe nonvocal behavior, a disadvantage insofar as nonvocal behavior could illuminate facets of defining a situation. But it is not overly presumptive to assume that unobserved physical gestures or facial expressions would be associated with silence and talk, of which we have a record. A second drawback is the possibility that a recorder stultifies the subject and so distorts the data he provides. To offset this, the recorder is going when S comes for the interview and while E repeats the solicitation which S has already heard, and upon which he volunteered. If a stultifying effect wears off, it should do so during this period. I can add the impression that subjects seem to get "unnaturally" stuck only when we would expect it and can account for it by the nature of our substantive purposes. Third, the laboratory is an "unnatural" scene and may distort everyday processes, but the paucity of previous work requires that we exercise the controls of artifice.

Form of Analysis

The form of analysis should be clear from the preceding discussion, but I will review it briefly here.

First, we shall determine the proportion of time devoted to emergence and relativity during order. This is a measure of the simple descriptive validity of the ideas in any exploratory study. It indicates which components occur, if any, and the amount of interaction devoted to them. This form of analysis *describes* the interaction.

Second, we shall attempt to isolate aspects which are important for the maintenance of order in a "causal" sense. We shall try to discover the influence of definition on the course of the interaction. Taking orderly interaction as a base, for example, we shall see how often each component appears as compared to how often it fails to appear. If theme is present most of the time during order, and absent most of the time during disorder, we can say it is important to order. Similarly, we can say that the absence of that component "causes" anomie.[9]

Third, we shall describe whole interactions as they run their course from order to challenge to anomie. We will array data side by side in order to provide a temporal description of what would otherwise be only cross-sectional pieces of the interaction.

Subjects

The sample includes thirty student volunteers, five for each of the yes-no splits. Such a sample is justified on conceptual and practical grounds. Conceptually, we seek means of definition that operate given a cultural baseline of interpretations. If we select subjects who are members of the same socioeconomic and subcultural group, it is less likely that differences in group membership will be confused with differences in definition itself. Practically, students are verbal and the procedure needs that kind of subject. Finally, this is an exploratory study that needs a laboratory setting, and the stubborn fact is that laboratory investigations, whatever their stage, must depend upon the captives we can get to come to the facility.

Summary

1. A random-answer procedure provides a partner to whom subjects can orient their behavior, thereby creating social interaction. However, the partner is designed to allow the subject to generate the overt activity

---

[9] Given that data are not much separated in time and extraneous factors are imperfectly controlled. I am sacrificing qualification of data for clarity of argument, on the assumption that the reader can do the former so long as he is sure about the latter.

of the interaction, thereby elevating the process of definition to the point of direct observation.

2. The random-answer technique permits an orderly interaction to be turned into an anomic interaction by splitting answers disproportionately and by giving contradictory answers.

3. Each component of emergency, relativity, and anomie has an observable corollary in the question-answer design. These corollaries serve as the manifest categories for analysis, and can be conceived as a set of coding instructions.

4. The whole design represents removal: Looking at emergence and relativity during order, disrupting the order to see if emergence and relativity disappear, and inferring the importance of emergence and relativity for defining the situation.

5. Implicit in the account so far are the following conditionals (although we will only be able to approximate the answers):

   a. Whether emergence and relativity are minimum values of social interaction.

   b. Whether emergence and relativity are coextensive.

   c. Whether anomie is reversible or irreversible.

   d. Whether the components of emergence and relativity are substitutable, in the sense that they are equally salient to definition.

One final remark. We have not stressed the elaborate statistical and laboratory controls which have come to be accepted as par for empirical investigations, but this does not make the study a soft meander across last resorts. Given the very substance of our conceptualization of defining the situation on one hand, and the primitive status of that conceptualization on the other, it would be baldly metaphorical to impose those controls here.[10] In our design, play between idea and observation is enhanced, but without allowing any observation all the possible connections to every idea. It neither decrees nor enfeebles connection. Rigor, then, has been accomplished in our case insofar as our empirical procedures and corollary observables are isomorphic with emergence and relativity, which would have been impossible had we adopted the standard techniques.

---

[10] That a measure imposes its own properties on a concept is a much more important point than I have suggested. See Clyde Coombs, "Theory and Method of Social Measurement," in Leon Festinger and Daniel Katz, eds., *Research Methods in the Behavioral Sciences* (New York: Dryden, 1953), Aaron V. Cicourel, *Method and Measurement in Sociology* (New York: The Free Press, 1964), pp. 1-37.

VII

Analysis

The questions formulated in the last chapter suggest our data should be organized in several independent ways. Emergence and relativity were proposed as specifications of the definition of the situation, and orderly laboratory behavior was devised to test them in a condition where definitions are likely to occur. Consequently, we must first observe orderly interaction to see if emergence and relativity are, in fact, empirically present, and, if so, how often. We shall array the proportionate amounts of behavior devoted to various components of emergence and relativity, and, thus, provide a concrete description of the interaction.

Because emergence and relativity are also supposed to be important for interaction, that is, necessary for it, orderly and anomic conditions were devised to test this supposition. We must observe orderly interaction to see not just whether emergence and relativity are present, but for how much of the order they can be said to *account*. We can do this by comparing their presence during order. We can do the same thing with the data on anomie, except that, in this condition, we expect behavior *not* to display emergence and relativity. Having a flow of interaction from order to anomie will provide us with some data that are separated in time and reduce the difficulty of inferring that one thing accounts for another from cross-sectional data alone. We will be able to follow the course of whole interactions from beginning to end.

Order

We will first inspect a single orderly protocol, along with a brief description of it, so that the reader will better understand the tabulations of

83

all protocols. Before summarizing the orderly interviews, we should see what a single interaction looks like. Codes are in capitals above the line.

ORDERLY PROTOCOL

Background

My problem's financing certain investments. I have some stocks, but not much, and I need insurance and a car. But I'll have to get a loan to cover all this, and face it, I'm a student. I'm not too sure how to go about it all. My father knows about this sort of thing, and I plan on getting advice from my bank manager in this regard. I'm not too sure they'll go for everything: car, stocks, and insurance. That's pretty much although it could be managed, because I work now and during the summers in a pretty good paying job. The stocks are always there, of course, so it's not spending money alone, but making it too. The car and the insurance are different. The car will depreciate and the insurance may not be necessary, except the insurance on the car. Anyway, that's my problem.

THEME
Q1. I have a problem financing certain investments in stocks, insurance, a loan, and a car. I plan to get some advice from my father and my bank manager. Do you think this is a wise approach to my problem?
A1. Yes.

SUBSTANTIVE CONGRUENCY
C1. I infer from your answer that you agree with my plan of action, getting advice from my father and bank manager. In a situation like this,
ELABORATION
it isn't smart to go ahead and commit yourself without talking it over with somebody more experienced and more objective. I mean there could be
REVELATION
reverberations that are full of trouble if things don't work out, and I can't see it the way another more experienced person would, so better not take a chance on that. I suppose anybody would do it that way.

THEME
Q2. Would you use the same general approach?
A2. Yes.

SUBSTANTIVE CONGRUENCY
C2. If you had the same problem, you'd follow a similar course of

ELABORATION

action. You're saying anyone could do this and make sense, regardless of

AUTHORSHIP

experience. Just like you told me it was the best approach, you'd use it
too, because it's always a good method to use regardless, to get somebody

MORAL REQUIREDNESS

else's opinion. You *should* get another idea, no matter how experienced.
Two heads are better than one. Of course, there's still the problem. I can
do a lot of things: loans, installments, that sort of thing. What should I
do?

THEME

Q3.   Do you think a bank loan is a wise course of action?

A3.   No.

C3.   I assume you're opposed to debt or loaning money from banks. I
might assume you're opposed to my loaning from a bank. Banks really

SUBSTANTIVE CONGRU-

collect the interest, and they make money on you. I agree with that; by

ENCY   ELABORATION

the time the interest is paid off, you've spent a lot of money. It's a good
idea to be leery of banks. Get somebody else's opinion but watch out for
banks. But where to get the money? It has to come from somewhere.
Maybe the insurance companies.

THEME

Q4.   What about an insurance company? Would that be wise?

A4.   No.

C4.   Hmm. Not an insurance company, huh? Well, I don't know what

FIT

to say. No bank, no insurance company. What's the reasoning here? He

AUTHORSHIP

says no bank loan and then doesn't think insurance companies are good

TYPICALITY

either. Maybe he's the kind of person who doesn't believe in loans. Loans
aren't too smart sometimes, since no matter where you get the money
there's going to be interest. Unless a friend gives it to you without asking

ELABORATION

for any extra. If I could get that kind of bargain—maybe from my father.

THEME

Q5.   Do you think I should approach my father about the loan?

A5.   Yes.

C5. That's it, you think I should approach my father about it because

REVELATION

a relative wouldn't ask for a loan with interest if he had the money to begin with. This way it would be possible to have more for the same

ELABORATION

amount of money. I could get more stocks or a better car. Or I could have the same thing for less money. I shouldn't get the money from banks or

AUTHORSHIP

insurance companies, but from a relative because you get more that way. The trouble is it might put a dent in my father's expenses, he's not real well off. I don't know if I should ask him.

THEME

Q6. Do you think I should ask my father even if it might be hard for him to raise it?

A6. Yes.

ELABORATION

C6. You're telling me to go ahead, my father would want me to do it this way because he would know it was better, and if worse came to worse we could always get a loan then, so it'd be the same difference anyway. I

MORAL REQUIREDNESS

wonder, though, if it's okay to put your father on the spot that way, just come right out and ask him for it even if he'd find it tight. A few dollars, maybe, but not enough for a car or stocks. I should at least get his ideas on it first.

THEME

Q7. Should I come right out and ask for it, without getting his ideas first?

A7. No.

SUBSTANTIVE CONGRUENCY

C7. I didn't think so. If I ask him for advice on the matter, he might

ELABORATION

come to see it would be best for him to loan the money himself instead of giving all that interest to the banks. That way, we wouldn't pay interest but it wouldn't put him on the spot either. But he might not see it either. What would I do then, if he doesn't see it this way? Should I bring it up then, or what?

Q8. If he doesn't see it that way himself, should I come right out and ask him anyway?

A8. Yes.

FIT

C8. Well, I don't know. That's interesting. I don't know what to make of that. I'm supposed to go ahead and ask him anyway. Because he won't see what I'm driving at? In case he doesn't realize it would be better not

REVELATION

to pay interest, I should bring it up. Fathers are like that sometimes, they don't really listen because their children seem like kids even after they're

ELABO-

mature, so I guess I should be careful to look out for this. If he doesn't

RATION

come up with the idea, go ahead and ask him, because he may not be paying attention, so I'd lose out on the best way of obtaining the loan if I

TECHNICAL EFFICIENCY

let it pass. That's a good idea, a good way to make sure everything has a

SUBSTANTIVE CONGRUENCY

chance to work out and not pay any interest. That makes sense. You

LIKELIHOOD

usually are making sense.

THEME

Q9. Do you think my father won't get the idea, so I'll have to bring it up myself?

A9. No.

C9. All that won't be necessary, my father will catch on even though it's

ELABORATION

good to take care of all possibilities in these things beforehand, just in case. Everything has a chance to work, all the angles, if it is thought over carefully beforehand. Let's see, it's still possible he'll get the idea but won't like it.

THEME

Q10. When he gets the idea, will he like it and want to loan me the money?

A10. Yes

C10. So it's all settled, he'll not only get the idea himself, he'll decide that it's the wisest course because there'll be no interest. I'm supposed to

AUTHORSHIP

let him bring it up, that's better than asking for it directly, and he'll think

ELABORATION

it's the best way. He definitely won't skip over it.

Summary

My investments can be financed, but not through banks or insurance companies. They charge interest that's too high and you end up paying them a long time before everything is paid up. When I ask my father for advice, he'll realize this and suggest that it'd be a wiser course to let him advance the money without interest. This is interesting. I didn't
                    ELABORATION
realize loaning money could be so easy once everything's planned out.
                                                         AUTHORSHIP
First, don't go to banks or insurance companies. Go to relatives. Then plan it out so the other guy gets the idea. I really feel I've been helped,
TYPICALITY   CAUSAL TEXTURE
psychiatrists know something. Talking things over makes you learn something about your situations. It's not that fathers don't want to help
                                                         REVELATION
out, that's not why you ask anyway. You ask them anyway because they may not be listening closely, even when they do want to help.

In his background, S is already beginning to construct the reasonable questions that he assumes will contain the fiat between E and himself. He states that he wants certain things, then makes them problematic with "but" and "although," balancing one against another in such a way that he can anticipate a line of questioning (investments, car, job, father) for the future. It is a rehearsal of the interview to come, a broad outline of the potential course of the interaction within which he expects the interview will develop. Substance is provided (car, investment) and latitude permitted (but, although).

S opens the questioning by asking advice about asking advice. He gets a yes answer, which is probably crucial for getting the interaction firmly started, because he anticipated it in the background. So he elaborates by saying "it isn't smart to go ahead and commit yourself," and that fathers and managers are "more experienced and objective." This in turn reveals to him that, because he is less experienced, some unknown trouble might arise unless he consults with those more experienced. The second question, answer, and comment all confirm this, to the point that it now becomes a moral imperative ("You *should* get another idea, no matter how experienced") to be involved with these questions and answers. Things are rolling.

S switches to the point of the problem, a loan, now that the idea of advice has been taken care of. He agrees with the no to Q3, which is not particularly surprising in light of the background. ("But face it, I'm a student.") He adds that "we should watch out for banks," then turns to insurance companies.

A4, no, pulls him up short. ("Hmm . . . Well, I don't know what to say.") Apparently he expected a yes. This surprise creates a search for fit ("What's the reasoning here?"), which is accomplished by typifying *E* as " the kind of person who doesn't believe in loans" because "there's going to be interest." He then elaborates a new wrinkle by entertaining the possibility of an interest-free "bargain" from friend or father. The agreement he gets on this from A5 keeps him going in his quest for a car, and in addition, makes other things possible as well ("more stocks or a better car"). But then he considers the possibility that his father, who appeared to have saved his chance for a car in C4, might not have the money. He wonders in Q6 if he should ask his father, because he might be hard-pressed to come through with the money.

He gets a yes in A6, and then plays off his father's sacrifice against his father's knowledge ("my father would want me to do it this way because he would know it was better"), a point that was established earlier in C1. But *S* is still not quite convinced that he should do it baldly, and agrees right away when A7 comes up no. It supports his doubt but doesn't ruin his chance. ("If I ask him for advice he might come to see it would be best. . . .") This reappears as the theme of the next question, Q8, as do most of the end parts of comments in this interview.

When *E* answers that *S* should ask directly if the father "doesn't see it that way himself," *S* is unsure. ("I don't know what to make of that.") But he finds a plausible referent by treating his father as an instance of all fathers. ("Fathers are like that . . . they don't really listen.") He then programmatically states what he has discovered throughout the whole interview. ("If he doesn't come up with the idea, go ahead and ask him, because he may not be paying attention, so I'd lose out on the loan if I let it pass.") *S* characterizes this "advice" as efficient and correct, and *E* as "making sense."

S continues in Q9 to ask about what his father will do with regard to what had previously been discovered in the interview. In Q8 *S* asks what he should do *if* his father "doesn't see it." Q9 asks what his father *will* do. That A9 suggests his father will see it without prompting enables *S* to treat the previous conversation as contingency planning to cover "all the angles."

Finally, in Q10, S takes the content of the interview as a potential outcome, as a potential factual order, by asking E to prophesy whether his father will like the idea. The answer is yes which permits him to treat the future as having already been accomplished ("It's all settled") by the program just developed in the interview. It is a precise and, to S, determinant formulation of what was merely a vague outline in the background. Some of the earlier possibilities had been eliminated and others sharpened, all with an eye to the future as a set of practical activities.

Thus, this orderly interview moves along from beginning to end with few pauses in the verbal behavior of S, while at the same time a more and more complicated structure of definition unfolds. S depicts what, for him, is a clearer scene in the summary than in the background—in his "understanding" of both the experiment and the substance of his problem, as when he states that he now "knows . . . interesting" and "helpful" things about banks and relatives, psychiatrists and talk. The subject, having made sense of the interview, leaves the laboratory with a feeling of received knowledge (there are seven declarative sentences in the summary). This definition is, of course, primarily a consequence of his own imposition of thematic meaning, because the answers are objectively senseless, that is, random. Moreover, that meaning is created at any single point by his anticipation of future answers ("I can do a lot of things . . . what should I do?") and reconstruction of past answers ("that's it" in C5 reconstructs the answer to Q4), rather than in the character of the immediate scene. The presumption of discovery, a presumption that S acts to fulfill by going right ahead in the face of one-word answers by an unseen experimenter, leads to the emergent revelation of fact; and, at the same time, the presumption of agreement tends to obviate the laboratory arrangements (one-word answers, being out of sight of one another, the tape recorder) that could have acted as barriers to definition. ("Well, I don't know what to say" is nevertheless accompanied by saying a great deal.) Bewilderment (fit) is rare and fleeting.

A summary of all orderly interviews appears in Table 1, which includes the amount of order in which emergence and relativity are present against the amount of order in which emergence and relativity are absent.

According to Table 1, emergence is present in 162 of the 181 units of order (89%), a sizeable majority, because this means it is absent in only 19 units (11%). Relativity, on the other hand, is present in only 76

TABLE 1. Presence-Absence of Emergence and Relativity
during Orderly Interaction*

	Present Percent (N)		Absent Percent (N)		Total Percent (N)	
Emergence	89%	(162)	11%	(19)	100%	(181)
Theme	86	(155)	14	(26)	100	(181)
Elaboration	71	(129)	29	(52)	100	(181)
Fit	26	(47)	74	(134)	100	(181)
Authorship	54	(98)	46	(83)	100	(181)
Revelation	34	(62)	66	(119)	100	(181)
Relativity	42%	(76)	58%	(105)	100%	(181)
Typicality	18	(33)	82	(148)	100	(181)
Likelihood	28	(50)	72	(131)	100	(181)
Causal texture	9	(16)	91	(165)	100	(181)
Technical efficiency	9	(17)	91	(164)	100	(181)
Moral requiredness	19	(34)	81	(147)	100	(181)
Substantive congruency	17	(31)	83	(150)	100	(181)

* (1) A single unit can contain any number of components, because subjects may utilize any number of meanings in one comment or summary (one question in the case of theme). They can, for example, address both the typicality and the fit of an answer within one comment or one summary. Once a component does appear, however, it is not counted again in the same unit. (2) Thus the (N) for overall emergence is 162, meaning that some component of emergence appears in 162 of the 181 units of order. (3) The total number of orderly comments and summaries is 181, that is, 181 comments and summaries have *not* been preceded by withdrawal of the psychotherapeutic reason for the experiment. (4) Because more than one component of emergence and relativity can appear in one unit of order, the sum of (N) for the components taken separately is greater than total (N).

of these units, or less than half the time. [1] Looking down the column on presence, we discover that emergence appears in slightly more than twice as many units (162) as relativity (76). Order in the aggregate is very like the order of the single interview we just discussed. A much greater

---

[1] As a check on the assumption that the interaction would be orderly up to the point where subjects withdrew their definition of the experiment as psychotherapeutic —that orderly and anomic conditions are, in fact, distinct—each unit of orderly behavior has also been coded according to the corollaries of powerlessness, meaninglessness, and innovation. Only 3 percent of the orderly units exhibited anomie, and these were omitted from the analysis.

proportion of orderly interaction is spent on emergence, specifically on drawing themes and elaborating them as new developments arise. Subjects stay on the original thematic track throughout the sequence of answers without giving much attention to anything else. Definition seems pushed ahead by the past and pulled ahead by the future, to the exclusion of other considerations. Actors do create a consistent set of meanings out of (potentially) disparate slices of interaction, primarily through being propelled by theme. Temporal continuity in meaning, attained by reconstructing what has happened and anticipating what will happen, commands more attention than contiguity across social space. The presence column describes these interactions. The absence column gives us a start on accounting for them. According to Table 1, when emergence appears the interaction is orderly.

However it is still a bit early to discuss further this concrete predominance of emergence, because there is little data at hand and our analysis of anomie is yet to come. I will hold that in abeyance for now, except to repeat that during order most meaning is created by incorporating the furbished past and anticipated future into their contemporaneous significance. Little use is made of the immediate scene itself. (Although the scene may be a substantive *object* of definition, it is not manifestly consulted in its own right, as a formulative mechanism of definition.) It should be obvious that these data tell us only that emergence and relativity are not coextensive in this single condition, not that emergence is more important than relativity. We cannot assert the importance of the one simply because it preoccupies the defining partner, any more than we can assume giving traffic tickets is more important than arresting thieves. It is quite possible, for example (and we have hypothesized as much) that both the mundane and the rare are necessary to continued interaction, just as both a random traffic pattern and unrestricted larceny would be disruptive, albeit in different ways. It is true that emergence describes a great deal of order, it being seldom absent in this condition. But it is quite possible that it is present during disorder as well. These alternatives can be clarified only after we observe the interviews in which anomie appears.

Anomie

Having been able to observe emergence—and relativity to some degree—during order, we must now look to their operation during anomie,

a circumstance in which they are expected to disappear. We have suggested in several places that definition is necessary to order. In accord
with this argument, we shall next observe anomie, which is the antithesis
of order. Bearing in mind that our data are cross sectional, that there are
few controls, and that numbers are small in some cases, the reader should,
nevertheless, be permitted a straightforward treatment of the data as
they reflect the basic argument that emergence and relativity are necessary to order. We can do this by comparing emergence and relativity
during order and during anomie. If they are absent in the latter condition,
the supposition that they are important to social order will be supported,
but if they are present, we must entertain the possibility that they are not
the crucial features we had thought. This would have to be our conclusion,
for example, if the tabulation for anomie is about the same as that already
presented for order. By the same token, to the degree that some components of definition are more often absent than others during anomie, we
may infer that they are more salient aspects of the definition of the situation than components that are present.

To make the ideas falsifiable, anomie shall be defined by the subject.
Any time he says the investigation is not psychotherapeutic in intent, or
substitutes some other purpose, the interview shall be called anomic and
behavior shall be studied for the absence of definition. In this test condition, we shall continue to code comments and summaries in terms of the
corollaries of emergence and relativity, in order to observe whether they
do disappear as expected. Furthermore, each expression of anomie (meaninglessness, powerlessness, innovation) will also be related to any present
component of emergence and relativity, should one show up in this
condition, thus providing a detailed analysis of definitional relations between order and anomie.

We shall now proceed with the causal status of emergence and relativity, which will be indicated by their absence during anomie. But an actual anomic protocol may make the analysis more meaningful, so I will
first present one and then discuss it briefly. The following subject withdraws the ostensible definition during C6.

ANOMIC PROTOCOL

Background

I've been attending the University of Miami, until I came up here this
year. Last year I met a girl down there and fell in love with her. I want to

marry her. However, my brother's met her and he thinks she's too bossy and it'd be a mistake if I married her. My father seems to like her, but my mother hasn't met her yet. I know she's right for me, but how can I convince my brother she is? My mother will make her decision when she meets her, but in the meantime my brother might say something that will influence her before then. My father doesn't talk to my mother, so he won't be any help. I really know she's right for me regardless of what anyone says, but I'll need the go-ahead of my family if everything's to go right.

THEME

Q1. My brother met the girl I love several months ago, but he doesn't think I should marry her. Should I try to show him she's changed, and will be all right to marry now?

A1. No.

C1. You mean I shouldn't try to convince him she's changed, once somebody makes up their mind about something like this there's no chang-

REVELATION

ing them. Especially my brother. It's no use even trying. People just hold on to what they believe no matter what, so I'm better off going ahead with another plan. But I still want to change my brother's mind. While it isn't

ELABORATION

easy to do this by just talking about it, maybe if he sees her he'll realize she's changed and isn't so bossy any more. I hope so.

THEME

Q2. Could I go about this, instead of telling him, by letting him see her and see that she's changed for himself?

A2. No.

ELABORATION

C2. You mean that she will be the same to him even if he sees for him-

AUTHORSHIP

self. No matter whether I tell him or he sees it for himself he won't want me to marry her, she'll be just as bossy as ever regardless of how she acts in front of him. Too bad I have a brother like that. Or are all brothers the same? The question is, will he change ever, or is there nothing I can do?

THEME

Q3. Will he ever change his feelings about her?

A3. No.

FIT
C3. Hmm. Really? This isn't easy to take, even though I can see what
AUTHORSHIP
you mean. You told me that it doesn't matter whether he is told, or even if
he sees her, he'll stick to his guns and always be against it. This means I
ELABORATION
can't go on worrying about what he thinks or changing his mind, but concentrate on seeing that he doesn't interfere. Of course, maybe he won't
ever change, won't ever like her and always think she's bossy, but still he
REVELATION
might realize it doesn't matter to me and I'm going to marry her whatever he says or thinks. He might figure it's no use and decide he can't do
anything about it either, just like I can't do anything about him. A truce
like that would be all right if he didn't keep objecting and say, "Go ahead,
there's nothing I can do to change your mind."

THEME
Q4. Even if he never likes her, will he decide it's no use doing all this
objecting and drop it?

A4. No.

C4. He won't drop his objections, but will keep on. That wouldn't be
ELABO-
very good, but it would still be possible to marry her and throw over the
RATION
whole family. Besides, my father seemed to like her, he doesn't have the
same opinion my brother does. And my mother hasn't met her yet, maybe
she wouldn't mind either. So there'd be only my brother to worry about
and he'd be outnumbered three to one. He always thinks he's right even
when everybody else disagrees, but so what? He'd just have to put up
AUTHORSHIP
with it. You say he'll never change his mind, but maybe that won't make
any difference.

THEME
Q5. Even though my brother disagrees, would the rest of the family go
along with the marriage?

A5. No.

ELABORATION
C5. They won't consent to the marriage. Well, there's nothing left but to
break off with the family. That'll be hard on everyone, but after all, I
REVELATION
love her and that's the most important thing. You don't go through life

with your brother, or your mother and father either. They must understand it's my problem and my decision, not theirs, and learn to live with
it. That's what I'll do. I hope they'll learn that I must marry her, loving
her like that. I mean it's all different when she's there, not like the home
life I've seen other places. If they don't want me to live my life like any
other normal person, they must pay the price by always being disap-
pointed. Maybe if I get a job paying good money and could support her,
they'd come around later.

THEME

Q6. If I got a good job with a good steady income, will they agree I
made the right choice?

A6. No.

LIKELIHOOD

C6. Christ, you keep saying no all the time. Maybe I can't . . . Maybe I
can't influence you either. I mean you keep saying everything I don't

WITHDRAWS DEFINITION

want to hear. I mean can this be psychotherapy? This can't be psychother-

CAUSAL TEXTURE

apy, I don't think. Not hearing the whole thing, you can't know what I'm
saying, must be hard to get the feel of it. This advice. I mean if it's true.

Q7. Do you want me to influence you in this conversation?

A7. No.

POWERLESSNESS

C7. (*15-second silence*) Well, maybe it's not put right. I can't make him
understand, know about my family that makes them different. These an-

TYPICALITY

swers, though, I don't know, psychologists must be pretty good to do this.
There aren't many who could. *this is appalling!*

Q8. You must be pretty good, aren't you as good as most psychologists?

A8. No.

LIKELIHOOD

C8. No. No. Wow, he doesn't think he's as good as most psychologists.
Wow. So what kind of advice is he giving? Bad advice. This can't be psychotherapy, I mean what kind of help is that? Do you think you're any

AUTHORSHIP

good, and he answers no. In fact, it's been no to everything I've said.
Hasn't it? Yes. Brother, family, changing their mind, everything. Maybe
it's no regardless.

Q9. Do you say no regardless?

A9. No.

C9. Well, that's good. I mean, what would that mean, saying no regardless? So what am I doing here in this room listening to him for? What is the purpose of this? Supposedly a simple method of giving advice. But
REVELATION
maybe it's supposed to be so simple even an incompetent psychologist can use it. That makes some sense. You can learn something about yourself
REINVOKES DEFINITION
just by talking about it. Maybe that is their reason here, to teach the person about himself just by getting things out of your system or something.
AUTHORSHIP
Then even if the advice is bad you know more. But don't follow the advice. I'll ask another question.

Q10. Do you think I should marry the girl?

A10. No.

C10. That must be it. They are trying to find a way of advising that teaches you more about yourself. That is what you are telling me. Even if
CAUSAL TEXTURE
I get bad advice, I will be better off because I will know myself better after
REVELATION
I'm finished. And if you know yourself, things will be easier all the way
ELABORATION
around. You will make better decisions. Like I know now for sure I'll marry the girl regardless of what my family says because it's so important to me. Before I came in here, though, I didn't know that, I wasn't sure about it and might have decided to forget her. So there's something to it. It might work.

Summary

For a while I was worried that this was a bad situation. I didn't know
FIT
how to take your advice when you said you weren't a very good psychiatrist, but then I realized it could still teach you something about yourself. I realized that I probably couldn't change my family about the girl, and I'd thought that over before. But I was especially helped when I realized that I should go right ahead with my plans because it is more important for me to live a happy life with the girl I love than an unhappy life with my

REVELATION
family. You don't live your life with your family anyway, you live it with
the person you marry, so that becomes more important later when you
mature. My family may come around anyway, after we're married; you
ELABORATION
can never be absolutely sure ahead of time about these things. It's always
a possibility. Very interesting. Even a poor psychiatrist can be helpful
if you just talk about yourself.

S withdraws the psychotherapeutic definition of the interview in C6.
Powerlessness appears in C7. He gets nothing but noes to all the question-
by-question actions he might take in dealing with his brother ("show
him," "letting him see," "the rest of the family," "getting a good job"),
as well as to his prognostication of the actual outcome ("will he ever
change?" "will he decide it's no use doing all this objecting?") These immediately precede withdrawal. It is not difficult to see that this is a product
of the *relation* between questions and answers, and of the relation between
S and E, when one considers what would have happened if he had received all yeses to the same questions. If, having received all yeses, he
would not have doubted his "influence" on E, as he does in Q7, we cannot
say it is the answers themselves that produce the result. That is, definition
is a shared rather than solo activity.

Series 9 is a revealingly comic phenomenon, one that occurs in a
few other interviews as well. S asks if E "says no regardless," which is
similar, but not quite identical, to Q7 ("Do you want me to influence you
in this conversation?"). When E answers no to "Do you say no regardless?" (Q9), S immediately comments "Well, that's good," fully ignoring
the import of his question, which is that this particular no could not be an
answer either. On the possibility that E's answers might not be responsive
to his questions, S asks about it. Then he treats the answer to his question
as if it were. The *logic* of Q9 entails that A9 is not an answer. The *action* in
C9 is that Q9 entails that A9 is an answer. $Q \subseteq A9 \neq A$, whereas the action in C9 is $Q9 \subseteq A9 = A$.

Among other things, this denial of purport—a purport, moreover,
of his own making and not imposed from without—recommends to us the
potency of the fiat of original definition. The original definition of the interview was psychotherapy. However, this S began to question the original
definition as grounds for acting on the answers, and we can say that the
interaction had gone beyond the vague boundaries of fiat between S and E

that were established by that definition. But then S takes anything at all as a sign for the original definition, and, in fact, proceeds to reinvoke it a few sentences later ("maybe that is the reason here"). It can only be said that the latitudes of fiat are what make anything possible. Fiat makes for definition and leeway at the same time.

There are several other items in this protocol that occur in other anomic interviews. We shall consider these in the remainder of this chapter: First, components of emergence and relativity are present; Second, relativity is present more often than emergence; Third, anomie gives way to order in some cases; Fourth, emergence and relativity are present less often in anomic protocols than in orderly ones.

Presence of Emergence and Relativity During Anomie

As in the previous section, units are comments and summaries. Once defined as something other than a search for therapy, comments and summaries will be treated as aspects of anomic interaction until and if the subject redefines the interview as psychotherapy, which is a possibility if we allow for temporary anomie. Table 2 summarizes the presence-absence of emergent and relative units during anomie.

TABLE 2. Presence-Absence of Emergence and Relativity during Anomie

Present (N)	Absent (N)
85% (127)	15% (22)

The data in Table 2 are not at all consistent with our conceptual supposition that emergence and relativity would be absent during anomie, because 85 percent of anomic comments and summaries exhibit one or another of their components. They are absent in only 15 percent, and therefore we must conclude that disorder includes elements of the definition of the situation. Anomic situations continue to be definable and significant, and are not jumbles of senseless chaos (unless emergence and relativity have nothing to do with sensibility). Emergence and relativity, devices which apparently help to define the social environment during order, continue, according to our test, during disorder, a seeming contradiction.

I question the def. "anomie"

These data demand explication. We shall have to return to the original conceptualization of the definition of the situation for ideas that might explain these findings, and then see if those ideas are compatible with observed laboratory behavior. Otherwise we would have to assert (1) the presence of emergence and relativity during order is a trivial matter, because they are also present during anomie; or (2) the paradox that anomie is orderly.

To begin with, recall the earlier discussion of anomie as a general notion that agglomerates diverse kinds of behavior. We distinguished between unintelligible purpose and unavailable means to clarify the idea. This led to a distinction between three expressions of anomie: (1) powerlessness, the description of one's own behavior as ineffectual; (2) innovation, the description of one's own behavior as unacceptable; and (3) meaninglessness, the description of purpose as unintelligible. Perhaps these specifications can explicate Table 3. Table 3 specifies the types of anomie associated with emergence and relativity.

TABLE 3. Presence of Emergence or Relativity
         by Type of Anomie

Type of Anomie	Percent Anomic Units Codable as Emergence or Relativity	Percent Anomic Units Not Codable as Emergence or Relativity
Powerlessness	71% (106)	00% (00)
Innovation	14 (21)	00 (00)
Meaninglessness	00 (00)	15 (22)
	85% (127)	15% (22)

According to Table 3, powerlessness and innovation account for the definitions existing during anomie, because meaninglessness is unaccompanied by any component of emergence or relativity. The latter represents the absence of definition we expected to find throughout all types of anomie.

Perhaps a meaninglessness protocol would be illustrative here. The following subject is trying to get into graduate school. In C6 the interview takes an anomic turn.

MEANINGLESS PROTOCOL

Background

I am hoping to go on to graduate school, to a good department of English. I have a scattered record. A's and C's. I believe my record is what it is because I do not apply myself. Oh, sometimes I study, but not consistently, not to the point where I always do my best. The C's show that, I think. They are C's in my major. My problem is whether I should go on to graduate school, and if I should, what I should do about it now.

Q1. I have a scattered record so far, but I would like to go on to graduate school. Should I?

A1. No.

C1. Well, yes, I suppose not. Though it does seem a bit too certain to flatly ignore the possibility that I have the ability, even if not the personality, to do the kind of work that graduate school requires. The A's are evidence that I *could* do the work.

Q2. I have several A's on my record, and shouldn't that recommend my ability to do graduate work?

A2. Yes.

C2. I have the ability, but I do not study. It is too soon to discount the possibility of graduate school. I am only a junior, so there is quite enough time to improve my study habits this year and next. Then, if I do so, my prospects would be quite good. At least one would have to say they would be quite good.

Q3. If I improve my study habits to the point where I bring up my grades, should I then go on to graduate school?

A3. No.

C3. My. Let's see. Scattered record, I shouldn't go on. No, wait a minute. Good grades, I have the *ability* to go on. There, that takes care of it. Not that I should go on—that I have the ability. Then I shouldn't go on anyway, even with the ability. I guess he's against graduate school. It is a long haul, and often leads to eunuchism.

Q4. I gather you are not for graduate school? Just a minute. Rather, are you in favor of graduate school?

A4. Yes.

C4. My. That's strange. I am being put on notice here. It is hardly clear. I shouldn't go on, even though I have the grades, and yet he is for graduate schools in principle. It must be something else. Something particular. Perhaps me. But it is difficult to understand just what. My personality? That is not supposed to be a criterion. Though it does enter in, I suppose. Falstaff would only have done well so long as no one saw him. Or heard him.

Q5. Is it my personality that makes you advise against graduate school?

A5. No.

C5. (*25-second silence*) This is obscure. Don't go to graduate school, though by any criterion I should. I want to, I truly do, I am the kind of person who could accomplish it, and I have the capacity. I find it hard to understand just what this advice is intended to convey. Perhaps he was mistaken in an earlier answer.

Q6. Have any of your earlier answers been mistaken? Would you like to change any of your previous answers?

A6. No.

C6. My God. This is utterly impossible. (*37-second silence*) Perhaps he is not a psychiatrist. Yes, I'll bet he isn't. Cruel. One can hardly expect this advice to be heeded. Heedless. The tender psyche an accessory to science. Worthless. I just don't know what to do.

Q7. Do you think your advice is worthwhile?

A7. No.

C7. Oh. No. Oh. (*57-second silence*) Well. No, huh? Geez, what am I doing here? He says his advice isn't worth a thing. What's he doing? I don't like this at all. Well, I'm supposed to say what he is telling me, but I can't. I don't know what the situation is. I don't know what he's telling me, I don't know what the situation is.

Q8. If your advice isn't worthwhile am I wasting my time and yours discussing the problem?

A8. Yes.

C8. (*52-second silence*) Well, then, what am I doing here? I don't know what's going on and I don't like it.

Q9. What's going on here? (*Experimenter silent because question cannot be answered yes or no*) I say, what's going on here? (*Experimenter silent*) Hey. (*Subject unplugs intercom between himself and the experimenter*) That can't be answered yes or no. (*43-second silence*) Still, he should answer it. Who's in there, anyway? Is it the same guy? (*Sub-

ject plugs in intercom) Are you the same person who was here at the beginning of this?

A9. Yes.

C9. Oh, I don't know. (*Subject plugs in intercom*) You better come in here. I'm finished. (*The post-interview discussion indicated that this last statement referred only to the experiment.*)

In C6, this subject withdraws his definition of the experiment as psychotherapy. ("Perhaps he is not a psychiatrist.") He proceeds to act on this by doubting the overall worth of the advice in Q7, an act which was preceded by giving *E* a chance in Q6 to amend one of his earlier answers. When *E* failed to take this offer, *S* began to doubt the whole affair.

There is hardly a search for theme in meaninglessness, nor are answers connected to one another in any way. Although the subject asks "What's going on here?" he does not then go on to compare answers in an attempt to connect these discrete aspects of his lab experience. He says something, but what he utters is more like noise than language, and in comparison with his previous orderly interaction, his actions are fragmentary, confused, and disconnected. The subject fails even to infer the existence of another, much less demonstrate that he can interact with him, and when he grasps at momentary strands of meaning they evaporate at a glance. He does not begin to address how typical the answers are of the experimenter, or the experimenter of psychotherapists, whether he could expect them on the basis of some previous action of the experimenter, what might be the causes of answers in terms of the experimental situation, whether they facilitate the goal of psychotherapy or any other goal, whether for moral reasons they "should" or "should not" have been given, or if they are substantively accurate in terms of his problem. Components of emergence and relativity, as formal mechanisms of interpretation, are characteristically absent during meaninglessness, and in this fragmentation of definition they correspond to a terminal state of interaction. According to these data, remove emergence and relativity and you replace social action with sheer stimuli, stimuli which do not implicate an intelligible relationship to the member.[2]

Having indicated that meaninglessness represents our original view that anomie will not exhibit any component of the definition of the situa-

---

[2] Max Weber, *The Theory of Social and Economic Organization*, trans. by A. M. Henderson and Talcott Parsons (New York: Free Press, 1964), p. 93.

tion, we must now turn to an examination of those data where emergence and relativity do appear. Within the framework of this investigation, anomie is a test condition of the necessity of emergence and relativity, and so if the latter appear during powerlessness and innovation, we cannot assert that they are the *sine qua non* of smooth and orderly interaction. On the other hand, their total absence during meaninglessness, a state in which sensibility disappears, does indicate they must be present in some degree if the interaction is not to come to a full stop. We must, therefore, ask if any distinctions at all exist between order on one hand and powerlessness and innovation on the other. Emergence and relativity may occur during anomie, but to a different degree than during order, a possibility we have not yet examined.

Table 4 summarizes the average number of definitional components present per unit of both anomic and orderly interaction, that is, the relative fertility of definition in anomic as opposed to orderly acts. Here we see that some component of emergence or relativity is observed 750 times in the 181 units of order, or slightly more than 4 times in each unit; and only 127 times in 149 units of anomie, somewhat less than once in each unit of powerlessness and innovation.[3]

TABLE 4. Average Number of Components Present per Unit of Orderly and Anomic Interaction

	Order	Anomie
Average Number of Components per Unit	4.14	0.84

This is a considerable difference in the expected direction. Because comments and summaries have been chosen as empirical units, and some component of definition appears in units that are powerless and innovating, the hypothesis that these states are barren of definition is not substantial. But neither are they as "full" as orderly interaction.

---

[3] Averaging meanings is hardly an adequate measure of the difference between order and anomie. It is intended metaphorically, to introduce the more appropriate analysis to follow. To take the average literally, one would have to show: (1) That for each degree of decrease in emergence and relativity there is a concomitant increase in anomie; (2) That the conceptual differences between emergence, relativity, and anomie are logically equivalent to differences in number.

Averaging for content is, of course, an incomplete way of dealing with our data, so we cannot yet come to any firm conclusions. We can say with confidence only that the ratio of meaning (component) to act (unit) is much smaller in the anomic case, and put off serious discussion of the matter until after we have also addressed the differences, if any, between the *kinds* of meanings that issue in order and anomie. We have discovered that the number of meanings diminish, and we now must ascertain if the quality of meaning changes as well.

The data in Table 5 point to the fact that anomie, by our criteria a meaningful state, is nevertheless meaningful in a different way than order.

As we have seen, the bulk of orderly interaction is devoted to linkage in time (74%), rather than to the setting (26%). But Table 5 shows that once subjects withdraw the original psychotherapeutic definition of the situation, that is, once the laboratory benchmark of disruption appears, they begin to address a greater proportion of their comments to relativity (68%) than to emergence (32%). There is a reversal of preponderance from emergence to relativity as the interaction shifts away from order, and so it is relativity that accounts for the presence of definition in two of the three types of anomie.

TABLE 5. Proportion of Observed Components Devoted to
Emergence or Relativity during Order and Anomie

	Order		Anomie	
Emergence	74%	(491)	32%	(41)
Relativity	26	(172)	68	(86)
Total Percent	100		100	
Total Observations		(663)		(127)

Now it is time to observe the presence-absence of all components of definition during anomie, just as we did for order in Table 1. We want to know, in detail, about the shift from emergence to relativity. We shall omit meaninglessness, because, as noted in Table 3, definition is absent in this state.

Two related matters are immediately noticeable in Table 6. First, when we take all components of relativity together, we find they are present in 68 percent in anomic comments and summaries (excluding meaninglessness). If we can say that emergence "causes" order, in the sense that it is present more often than not in this condition and absent more often than not during anomie, then by the same token we must say that these data recommend that relativity "causes" anomie. Emergence is present 89 percent of the time during order and only 32 percent of the time during disorder. Relativity, on the other hand, is present 42·percent of the time during order and 68 percent during anomie.

TABLE 6. Presence-Absence of Emergence and Relativity
            during Anomic Interaction

	Present Percent (N)		Absent Percent (N)		Total Percent (N)	
Emergence	32%	(41)	68%	(86)	100%	(127)
Theme	05	(7)	95	(120)	100	(127)
Elaboration	00	(0)	100	(127)	100	(127)
Fit	03	(4)	97	(123)	100	(127)
Authorship	11	(14)	89	(113)	100	(127)
Revelation	11	(14)	89	(113)	100	(127)
Relativity	68%	(86)	32%	(41)	100%	(127)
Typicality	16	(20)	84	(107)	100	(127)
Likelihood	08	(11)	92	(116)	100	(127)
Causal texture	25	(32)	75	(95)	100	(127)
Technical efficiency	08	(11)	92	(116)	100	(127)
Moral requiredness	04	(5)	96	(122)	100	(127)
Substantive congruency	05	(7)	95	(120)	100	(127)

The second matter, and a helpful one, is the *distribution* of the *components* of relativity: No one component appears in more than 25 percent of the cases, and most of them are present in less than 10 percent. Causal texture appears in 25 percent of the 127 anomic units, typicality in 16 percent, and so on to moral requiredness, which appears only 5 times out of a possible 127. Moreover, taken singly, components of relativity are in evidence about as often in the anomic condition as they were in the orderly condition (Table 1). This is a reflection of the thinness of anomic definition we discovered in Table 4. Anomie, unlike order, is sparsely defined. Anomic comments and summaries display some definition, although not much, certainly nothing like the full serving characteristic of order. Moreover, the fabric of anomic definition is predominantly relative (68%), a reversal of the orderly case. Anomic definitions are few and relative; orderly units contain a much expanded variety of meaning, and this expansion is due to the greatly increased relevance of emergence for order. It is emergence which decreases as the interaction shifts from order to anomie (from 74% to 32%), whereas relativity continues apace.

Anomie is not devoid of meaning. Relativity appears quite regularly when we take one component of definition per unit as a criterion, so we cannot say that our expectation that anomie would be empty has been demonstrated. But anomie differs from order in two respects: Definitions are meager in number, and those that do exist are relative ones. A drastic decrease in emergence, accompanied by about the same amount of relativity, is a distinguishing feature of anomie. Further on we shall consider this finding insofar as it can be used to compare the influence of definition on order and anomie.

In attempting to account for these observations with regard to our original ideas about the character and necessity of definition, we might begin with a reappraisal of emergence and relativity. Although they do not disappear during anomie, they can be used to distinguish between anomie and order, because the components of one are replaced by the components of the other as the interaction shifts. Perhaps implicit differences between emergence and relativity, then, can explicate the empirical shift from one to the other, and perhaps that difference can help to describe how definition remains as the situation takes a disorderly turn.[4]

Returning to the discussion of emergence and relativity in Chapter I, we may begin our reappraisal by noting a tacit but important distinction between them: Persons *assess* their environments in terms of relativity (typicality, likelihood, etc.), whereas they *assume* there will be certain emergent properties of the interaction (theme, fit, etc.). Consequently, we might ask if making assessments entails the same behavior as making assumptions, with the expectation that it does not, for empirically assumptions of emergence predominate in one condition (order), and assessments of relativity in the other (anomie). The first occurs when outcome

---

4 The reader should be warned here, as elsewhere, that two of the conditions that obtain in this test are atypical of some routines in daily life. First, *E* is supposed to be an expert, and *S* may hang on his every word. Results would probably be different among equals. Second, being unable to see *E* and getting one-word answers are a very unusual form of interaction. Just how the latter affects definition is problematic: It could amplify the tentativeness by supplying so little to go on, or it could solidify definition for the very same reason. Some of these matters are taken up below.

neatly follows the script; the second when there is a discrepancy between
script and outcome.

We shall begin to answer these questions by depicting possible differences in the ways assessment and assumption influence behavior, and then
inspect the data more closely:

1. Assumptions (sometimes invidiously called preconception, bias,
set) about what will occur, and which are not called into doubt as the
interaction proceeds, may obviate manifest assessments. Assumptions that
are substantiated in the course of interaction may *predecide* potential
assessments, in which case typicality, likelihood, and the other components
of relativity are not directly consulted during order. One need hardly notice the supermarket clerk or the wife in these instances, as long as the
groceries are bagged or the cheek pecked, as one assumes they will be
before the transaction begins. One assumes they will be done, and takes
the appearance of their having been done as enough. Because the original
agreements that generate the interaction go unquestioned during order,
they predominate because the actors are given no reason to do anything
else. Here defining the situation remains a temporal action in which immediately occurring events are incorporated into preceding ones, and into
those which the agreements create as the future. The original agreements
generate their own thruway documentation. Meanings are documented,
elaborated, placed within the original context over and over again, and, in
this respect, are indigenous to themselves.

2. Assumptions that do not seem borne out, which are instead called
into doubt during challenge and disruption, make it necessary for the actor
to *emphasize* assessments if he is to discover just what is happening to the
situation. Such dubious assumptions may require falling forward into the
immediate situation in order to rediscover or maintain the sensibility of
the interaction; where else can the surprised man go but to the immediate
present, to the assessments of relativity? If the clerk doesn't bag the
groceries, or the wife peck the cheek, the appearance no longer recommends the assumption. Where does one look for bearings? The routines seem to be faltering, so it can hardly be the routines that need to be
consulted separately from the thing at issue. One now glances at the clerk,
peers at the wife. Surprises and contradictions confound the presumed
agreements, and, because they happen in the present, must be tested by
assessing the here and now situation. This would have to be the new focus
of definition because, on one hand, the current condition of things is the

locus of surprise, and, on the other, because the presumed agreements have led to this.

3. The outcome of this assessment, which can be positive or negative, will determine whether the interaction is orderly or anomic. Once assessment begins, subjects can define the interaction as typical or atypical, with or without causal texture, moral or immoral, and so on. What is she doing? Do other clerks typically do this? Is there something in the wife's day that caused it? What else is happening in the situation—is she busy, having a heart attack, or what? Furthermore, what *should* she be doing? In other words, are these "good reasons," in the sense that they can be called typical, adequately caused, correct? Upon these decisions will depend the orderly or anomic quality of the interaction.

It is reasonable that assumptions can go unquestioned during an interaction that is not disrupted, because in this case there would be no need to bother addressing particular matters already taken care of by the assumptions. Here interaction would display an inertial direction in which the concrete details of the immediate scene remain taken for granted, unauthenticated by surveillance activity on the part of the subject. Disruption, a challenge to the original assumptions of emergence, leads to an effort toward resolution, and proceeds by directly reconnoitering immediate objects in the scene. Correspondence between sign and meaning—the process of inference—moves from certainty to doubt, and leads to a consideration of the phenomena that, when everything had been going smoothly, was plainly assumed and never questioned. If this relative assessment is positive, order will continue, but if it is negative, order will be transformed into anomie. In other words, the meaning of the situation will be pursued across the boundaries of social space when disruption occurs because this dimension is the only alternative when the assumptions of emergence are cast into doubt. Following this, the orderly or disorderly form of the interaction is associated with the positive or negative result, respectively, of that pursuit.

Now how might the data shed empirical light on these suggestions? First, Table 1 has already made it clear that the assumptions of emergence are the focus of definition during orderly interaction. The ostensible purpose of the experiment is to find a simple method of psychotherapy, and as long as subjects maintain this definition of the experimental situation, the assumptions of emergence dominate the interaction. They continue in this condition to find the theme of the original assumption (psychotherapy) by asking questions that bear on the substance of their problem; they elaborate the problem in accordance with the assumption that, because it is psychotherapy, they are in fact being given advice; particular answers are fitted into the theme, and are explicitly connected in meaning to other answers; and subjects find a revealing event around which they construct their answers. These components of emergence preoccupy the interaction, and, because they contain the assumptions to be borne out, they are rather casually documented as the interview runs its course.

Conversely, anomic interaction is pervaded by relative assessments of the situation. Subjects begin to question typicality, likelihood, causal texture, technical efficiency, moral requiredness, and substantive congruency more often, thus reversing the preoccupations of order. According to these data, disruption of the ostensible reason for the relation between subject and experimenter supervenes between documenting assumptions and the more finite work of defining the outward milieu in which those assumptions seem to be failing.

The data so far presented do not refute our suggestion about the relation between emergence and relativity as one between assumption and assessment, up to the point where subjects conclude their assessment either positively or negatively. Here we propose that anomie accompanies negative outcomes when subjects consult the components of relativity. Table 7 presents outcomes for orderly and anomic interaction. Positive outcomes are those where subjects decide that an attribution is typical, likely, and so on, whereas negative outcomes are those called atypical, unlikely, and so forth.

Table 7 indicates that outcomes during orderly interaction are usually positive (84%), but during anomie they are negative (75%), thus supporting our earlier speculation. Subjects in an anomic environment find it atypical, without causal texture, technically inefficient, lacking in morality, and in disagreement with their own view of accuracy. The only exception is that they find events likely as often as not. Resolution of the challenge created by disrupting the original definition is thus associated with positive outcomes, anomie with negative ones, as subjects address the various components of relativity.

Summarizing the presence and absence of emergence and relativity during anomie, the data suggest the following:

1. Emergence and relativity operate during powerlessness and innovation.

TABLE 7. Positive and Negative Outcomes
during Order and Anomie

	Positive Percent		Negative Percent		Unresolved* Percent		Totals	
Relativity during Order								
Typicality	88%	(29)	9%	(3)	3%	(1)	100%	(33)
Likelihood	96	(48)	4	(2)	0	(0)	100	(50)
Causal texture	75	(12)	19	(3)	6	(1)	100	(16)
Technical efficiency	65	(11)	29	(5)	6	(1)	100	(17)
Moral requiredness	88	(30)	3	(1)	9	(3)	100	(34)
Substantive congruency	77	(24)	23	(7)	0	(0)	100	(31)
Totals	84%	(154)	13%	(21)	3%	(6)	100%	(181)
Relativity during Anomie								
Typicality	10%	(2)	65%	(13)	25%	(5)	100%	(20)
Likelihood	45	(5)	45	(5)	10	(1)	100	(11)
Causal texture	6	(2)	78	(25)	16	(5)	100	(32)
Technical efficiency	0	(0)	100	(11)	0	(0)	100	(11)
Moral requiredness	0	(0)	100	(5)	0	(0)	100	(5)
Substantive congruency	14	(1)	86	(6)	0	(0)	100	(7)
Totals	12%	(10)	75%	(65)	13%	(11)	100%	(86)

* A case is unresolved when a category is consulted but there is no resolution either positively or negatively.

2. Their presence in these states stems from a basic distinguishing characteristic that we did not fully conceptualize in the beginning. Then we described them as two similar phenomena except for their respective concern with time and space. Now we find that emergence and relativity also differ in their concern with assumption and assessment, a difference that is reflected in laboratory preoccupation with emergence during order, and with relativity during anomie. We have suggested that this happens because assessments seldom need to be invoked until interaction calls assumptions into doubt. During orderly interaction, subjects take relativity for granted by honoring the appearances of emergence. Explicit "verification" is unnecessary.

3. Once the original definition is challenged, and subjects find it necessary to assess their situation in terms of relativity, order continues when that assessment is positive, but anomie arises when it is negative.

Discussion

Chapter I suggested that the purely physical metrics of chronological time and geographical space must be overcome if there is to be interaction. It also suggested that emergence and relativity transform these physical metrics into social ones. Now our data indicate that two kinds of anomie include emergence and relativity. Our original ideas require modification.

Remember the basic argument that persons proceed through social interaction on the basis of vague agreements that their environments are communal ones, a broad fiat that permits a great deal of latitude in specific detail and makes it unnecessary for actors to continually check on the correspondence between an agreement and an action. Our concepts, our thinking about the world, have an "open texture" because they are essentially incomplete. The vague agreement that they will observe comparable events provides a general arena within which persons go about linking specific substantive details through time and across space, so that they can participate with one another and communicate that participation on the level of interaction. Getting down to cases, it would seem that emergence is the guide of vague agreement. Emergence, now the mechanism of agreement, sustains the substantive assumptions that interacting partners bring into a social situation. It embodies the accessory fiats that are documented through the course of orderly social exchange. Take a love affair, for example, and grant that each lover thinks the other loves too. Now do these kinds of lovers, so long as they meet this criterion, routinely make their affair problematic? They may hope it won't end, and in this sense they may be said to wonder or even expect that it might end at some future point, but should this be so it too is emergent because it is an assumption. And the dimmer the point in the future, the more open the texture of their affair with regard to its termination. As long as particular acts do not contradict these original agreements, emergence is self-maintaining and there is little activity devoted to checking out the environment in detail.

When discrepancies arise, however, actors reconnoiter the immediate scene to see if those original agreements, largely presumed, can in fact be used to define the interaction. When things turn out to be not what they seemed, they seek materials for redefinition. Suppose one lover suspects that it is only infatuation. What does he do? Perhaps he checks on the typicality of the other—whether the other is the "type" for love or infatuation. Or he might wonder if the other actually agrees with the *correctness* of the assumption that it is love. He might discover that, morally speaking, the expression of physical attraction was lust rather than love, and so forth. In this case, circumstantial details of the environment recommend their own accord or discord with the original assumptions. Relativity is an activity of studied reckoning, considerably different than documentation of fiat. The former is a concentrate, more volatile than assumption documenting, in that it produces the positive and negative outcomes that are empirically related to anomie. Quine may have had relativity in mind when he said that "Good purposes are often served by not tampering with vagueness."[5]

We shall next examine associations between emergence, relativity, and anomie. Because components of definition appear during anomie, we shall investigate these relationships in some detail and try to connect the similarities and differences between the various kinds of disorder we have just discovered.

Relations Between Components
of Emergence, Relativity, and Anomie

Table 6 indicates that different components of definition accompany different anomic states. We must conclude that anomie includes many varieties of behavior as far as the definition of the situation is concerned. Powerlessness and innovation are so different that the only component they have in common is revelation. Meaningless, equally distinctive, is without any component of emergence or relativity.

We shall begin with the following powerless segment of an anomic protocol. The subject is "lavaliered" (pinned) to a boy in another state; she wants to date at school, and doesn't know if she should tell him.

Q5. Should I write and tell him that when he does come back to school I'll date him?

A5. No.

C5. Well, maybe that's all right, seeing you told me before. But I don't know. Still, this discussion is pretty one-sided, I mean you can't know enough about this. Of course, if I am going to date somebody now, maybe I'll be dating someone when he comes back to school. What a mess. I can't write him, can't send back the lavalier. I can't really tell what you think. Maybe you think I should forget him. I wonder what this really is?

Q6. Should I forget about him and not even write?

---

[5] Quine, *Word and Object*, p. 127.

A6.　Yes.

C6.　Aha. You want me to be heartless. No writing at all, just drop him. Isn't that just like a psychiatrist? After all, we went together for some time and now I am to drop him without a word or any kind of explanation. He is not stupid, you know. He would understand—I hope—he'd understand why I do it. He might not agree, but I owe him that.

Q7.　Don't you think I should write and try to explain why I think it's best for both of us?

A7.　No.

C7.　Why not? This advice can't be good because it doesn't let anything be explained. I mean, how does he know how important it is? Can't talk to him or show why. He may even be told before he comes back to school, and would that be a surprise. Fraternity brothers, friends, people like that. It doesn't matter what I think, though, he is going to go ahead with this advice.

In this interview challenge and withdrawal of ostensible purpose occur when the subjects asks, "I wonder what this really is?" She entertains the possibility that the presumed original agreement and the actual facts of the case do not coincide. With this remark, this unit and all succeeding ones are treated as anomic. That powerlessness is the particular state is indicated when she asserts "It doesn't matter what I think, he is going ahead with his advice." In general, powerless subjects:

1. Continue to author a search between answers. ("Seeing you told me that before.")

2. Depict a revealing motif for particular answers. ("Of course, if I am going to date somebody now, maybe I'll be dating someone when he comes back to school.")

3. Assess the experimenter's typicality by providing him with group membership. ("Isn't that just like a psychiatrist?")

4. Locate causes of their observations in experimental conditions. ("Can't talk to him or show why.")

5. Address the instrumental efficacy of the interview. ("This advice can't be any good because it doesn't let anything be explained.")

On the other hand, powerless subjects seldom:

1. Find a theme.

2. Elaborate it, even if they do find one.

3. See answers and other activities of the experimenter as likely or unlikely.

4. Deal with the morality of the experimenter's behavior.

5. Discuss the empirical accuracy of answers.

Note the subject's references to the situation when she remarks that it makes discussion one-sided, thwarts explanation, and prohibits conversational talking to the experimenter in order to show him what's what. This is generally the case for powerless anomie, where reference is to causal texture more often than any other component. Causal texture, a component which invokes the architecture of the experiment, defines the laboratory procedures as barriers that foil the subject's attempt to control outcomes, that is, as a *situation veto* of the original agreement. (During innovation there is an absence of this type of definition and instead a characterization of the experimenter's *intentions* as the creator of subjects' dilemmas.) If we think of subjects as having two kinds of objects in their environment, an interacting partner and a set of external conditions, powerless subjects are absorbed in the walls between themselves and their partner, the conditions created by impersonal rules, which they conceive as obviating the goals of the partners. Concentration on the structure of the maze, rather than on the persons within it, leads the powerless to conclude that the events of the interaction are situationally produced.

Even typicality, when used, has an impersonal ring: "Isn't that just like a psychiatrist?" rids the act of its fully personal taint, for here the meaning of individual behavior is found in group ties. Together with causal texture, this emphasis is a way of defining acts emanating from individuals as involuntary.[6]

Turning now to innovation, we shall find it very different from powerlessness. In the following protocol, the subject wants to know what she should do to prevent her divorced mother from remarrying: the experi-

---

[6] This situation orientation may exemplify the difference between mechanical and organic solidarity. Durkheim depicts the first as creating among members a normative emphasis on individual responsibility for one's own acts, whereas organic solidarity induces the view that individual behavior stems from circumstances beyond one's control. If subjects come to the laboratory as if the interaction were an organic one between expert and client, assessment would stress inexorable conditions rather than personal control. And it is the latter, according to Durkheim, that makes possible the attempt to restore the status quo ante rather than to "repressively" punish the offender. *On the Division of Labor in Society*, pp. 70-200.

menter has told her to do several different things, and she has already suspended the psychotherapeutic definition of the interview:

Q6. Do you think it's right to be so sure about things, using this method where you don't know much?

A6. Yes.

C6. Phooey. This'll never work. Not with his kind of advice.

Q7. Do you think this method will work? I mean, you agree that it probably won't work, don't you?

A7. Yes.

C7. Sure. He tells me it's right to be sure, then he says the method won't work. He is liable to do anything. So why am I doing this, if it won't work? Somebody told me about these people once. He's not doing a simple method of advice at all, it's probably something entirely different.

Q8. Are you doing something else, something entirely different than a simple method of psychiatry?

A8. Yes.

C8. Uh-huh. So. He's not doing psychiatry. What's he doing then? Why did he tell me yes when I asked that? Well. I'm not going to go along pretending it's something it's not. I don't care what he's up to, I'll just go along and ask the same questions over again. Who cares? *(Subject restarts the interview, asking the same questions she had at the beginning until she has asked ten questions altogether.)*

This subject clearly indicates the innovating character of her responses when she says "I don't care what he's up to. I'll just go along and ask the same questions over again. Who cares?" The institution of contract having broken down as she withdraws the psychotherapeutic definition of the interview, she can merely follow the formal letter of the instructions, and do no more than literally conform to the *ad hoc* agreements between subject and experimenter that those instructions represent.[7] When subjects innovate they:

1. Reveal a referent for answers, and are similar in this respect to the powerless. ("Somebody told me about these people once.")

2. Establish answers as likely. ("He is liable to do anything.")

---

[7] *Ibid.*, pp. 214-215 ff. With regard to tape recorders as stultifying, note that this subject says what she does with full knowledge that there is a permanent record of her remarks.

3. Assess the empirical accuracy of answers. ("Phooey. This'll never work.")

Note the high proportion of comments devoted to the experimenter himself, rather than to the structure of the experiment. References to "him" as the perpetrator of answers contrasts with the structural referent of powerlessness. She blames the *intentions of the experimenter* for the experimental state of affairs, whereas *situation vetoes* are the culprits of powerlessness. During innovation, the relation is conceived as between the subject and an unworthy experimenter, and is unrestricted by the situation, so the subject is able to deem any behavior not only appropriate, but possible. She can thus plot a device to finish the interview and leave the scene. Powerless anomie, on the other hand, is more constraining, because it incorporates a definition that does not permit subjects to manipulate the system of the interview itself.

Thus, general anomie has a very different structure of definition than order, and its specific subdimensions are equally distinctive. When the assumptions that bind partners in orderly interaction are disrupted, emergence is replaced as the mechanism of definition by relativity, and the interaction moves toward anomie. In the latter state, moreover, a variation in the components of emergence will be accompanied by a variation in the kinds of anomie. During orderly interaction, the bulk of activity consists of documenting original assumptions throughout the span of the interaction, and meaning consists of the creation of pasts and futures. During anomic interaction, however, meaning emanates from consulting the relative here and now, the present, when definition is invested in either the situation or the other person (except for meaninglessness, which is without definition). These consultations, conceived as a relationship of definition between partners correspond to the various disjunctures we call anomie.

For those with a psychological bent, there may be chance results of psychological predispositions. Those who become partners in anomic interviews may simply bring these tendencies into the laboratory, a possibility we shall briefly address below.

Attitudes and Anomie

Each subject is administered a Srole scale at the beginning of the interview, and his score on the scale will represent attitude or predisposition.[8] To the degree laboratory reaction varies independently of his score, we can more surely infer that laboratory disruption of definition is creating the effect we intend, and not some predisposition the subject plays out when he comes to the laboratory.

Because we are not interested in differentiating individuals by internal scalar differences in Srole score, we shall use the method of summated ratings rather than Guttman's scalogram analysis. This procedure relaxes the criteria of scalability, and increases the possibility that predispositions will have an effect on the laboratory interaction. A higher score is the result of greater agreement with anomic statements and indicates greater attitudinal anomie. Table 8 presents the distribution of scores.

On absolute grounds, over half the subjects score "1" by the method of summated ratings, which is low, so we cannot infer that they are basically or fundamentally anomic in attitude. But let us stack the cards according to the possibility that any degree of attitude, however slight, might trigger an anomic response in the laboratory. The salience of definitional disruption would, in this case, be tested by the relation between score, whatever it might be, and anomic response to laboratory disruption.

TABLE 8. Scores for Srole Scale Items

Score	Subjects
0	1
1	16
2	7
3	5
4	1
5	0
Total	30

A total of seventeen subjects are engaged in anomic interaction at some point during the experiment. Table 9 presents the score distribution for these subjects.

Table 9 relates scale scores to experimental anomie in the familiar fourfold table.

---

[8] Srole, "Social Integration and Certain Corollaries: An Exploratory Study," pp. 709-716.

TABLE 9. Relationship between Srole Score
          and Laboratory Anomie

		Experimental Anomie		
		Yes	*No*	*Total*
Srole Score*	High	2	4	6
	Low	15	9	24
	Total	17	13	

* Srole scores dichotomized into high and low, cutting points between two and three.

According to these data, there is no positive relationship between internal attitude, measured by Srole's items, and laboratory responses to the disruption of definition. Only two of the six persons with higher scores respond anomically during the experiment, whereas fifteen of those with lower scores respond anomically. We may say with some assurance (omitting the fact that the N is small), that the constellated presence-absence of emergence and relativity is not spuriously associated with laboratory anomie, in the sense that this association occurs independently of the internal attitudes people carry around with them. The disruption of meaning, as an aspect of relations between actors, seems to produce the effect. This is not so extraordinary; we are only saying that the sociological character of the laboratory interaction is social.

We shall now move on to the final third of the analysis, a description of the interview as it moves through the various forms of order and anomie.

Order, Anomie, and Reorder

Because the unexpected appearance of definition during anomie has already required a discussion of the flow of the interview during order and disruption, this section will emphasize the dynamics of interaction once anomie has occurred. The overall configuration is as follows:

```
                                    7 Powerless  ⟶  2 Reorder
30 Order  ⟶  17 Powerless  ⟨       5 Innovation ⟶  0 Reorder
                                    5 Meaningless ⟶  3 Reorder
```

Curiously, the behavior immediately following disruption and challenge is always powerlessness.[9] Upon withdrawal of the original definition of the situation, assessments are accomplished in terms of causal texture and typicality, after which all three forms of anomie turn up about equally. Note, too, that reorder occurs in five cases. These subjects reinvoke the original definition of the experiment as psychotherapy, with the result that here anomie is only temporary. The dynamics of anomic interviews exhibit a phased mobility between types that, in terms of our concepts, operate as follows:

PHASE 1: *Order.* Emergence predominates here. The emphasis is upon documenting the assumption of theme, elaborating the theme, and working to fit discrete observations into the theme. Compared to anomie, this activity is prosaic and workaday, even somnolent. Subjects follow a linear path toward psychotherapy in the discussion of their problem, link past comments together and routinely anticipate that it will be further explicated in a predictable future.

PHASE 2: *Challenge.* Contradictory answers, and answers that are all alike, infect the comments of subjects, and the original assumption that they are helping to discover a simple method of therapy is questioned. The fiat of mutual purpose is no longer taken for granted, and subjects formulate their doubt by shifting the focus of definition to assessments of relativity.

PHASE 3: *Powerlessness.* The outcome of assessments are predominantly negative, and are concerned with aspects of the situation that are conceived as having vetoed the possibility of therapy.

PHASE 4: *Powerlessness, innovation, and meaninglessness.* Some subjects spin off from powerlessness into meaninglessness and innovation. The latter stresses likelihood and congruency, components that emphasize the intentions of the experimenter rather than the structure of the situaion. Meaninglessness exhibits no mode of definition at all.

PHASE 5: *Reorder.* In some cases, anomie proves temporary. Three meaningless and two powerless subjects cease assessing their situa-

---

[9] Most likely a consequence of the "expertise" of *E*. Powerlessness is probably a first result of unsatisfactory relations with a superordinate. It enables *S* not to question *E*'s general competence, hence preserving the notion of common membership in *something*, even though withdrawal of the ostensible purpose has eliminated psychotherapy.

tion and reinvoke the original definition of the interview as psychotherapy, proceeding once again to emergence and the fiat of agreement. Most
anomic subjects, however, do not reinvoke order. None of the innovators
do so. *by definition, no ?*   *how could it be of innovation? in its aspects ?*

Clearly, anomie is not social death. It was apparent in our analysis of
salience that components of definition can exist in two of the three anomic
states, and now we discover that change occurs, and can be described, even
after anomie begins. Anomie is thus progressive in two senses—it can
change in type, and it can change back to order. Is there any reason for
this, some behavior that can put ideas as well as arrows between phases?
The concepts here have not been developed to account for trends between
trends, and so interviews cannot be coded except by anomic, emergence,
and relativity. However, we can chance a few speculations.

First, innovation does not change. A possible artifact of the small
number of cases, this may also be because innovation is the only state accompanied by positive outcomes in the assessments of relativity. Half of
the outcomes of likelihood are positive, and in an interesting way, for they
are positively *ad hominum*. One subject, for example, states that "He will
say anything, I can see that," when referring to the experimenter. Perhaps
there *is* a discovered pattern for innovators, our concepts notwithstanding,
that grows out of the subject's characterization of the other person. Can
there be an anomic pattern, one that is a positive outcome in that it is
called likely by those involved?

We may start by distinguishing between various kinds of normative
violation, challenge, or discrepancy in terms of their effects on the definition of the situation. One kind of violation is that which, although not
actually anticipated, *could* have been according to the whole normative
order of interaction. Sociologists who study these violations are usually
interested in "societal reaction to deviance,"[10] a phrase that implies that
some surprises are not merely tenable for actors, but even likely from
their point of view.

In this circumstance, there is a first point at which the actor may be
surprised and his definition challenged, but the surprise then is absorbed

---

[10] *See* Edwin M. Lemert, *Social Pathology* (New York: McGraw-Hill, 1951) ;
Howard S. Becker, ed., *The Other Side: Perspectives on Deviance* (New York: The
Free Press, 1964), pp. 87-178. These studies, though promising, are still less than
complete. Yet to be described are: (1) The relation between the normative order and
the kinds of labels it provides, and (2) Just what is being reacted *to*, independently
of the reaction itself. In the second case, a study of both labeled actions and labeling
reactions is necessary.

into a change of definition. The change makes it possible for him to expect such behavior, with the result that, being likely, it is no longer surprising. These are routine violations for which the social system regularly
makes allowances. Once the membership decides a violation did in fact
happen, it provides ready-made labels and sanctions. There are many examples of this, from the *faux pas* to murder, which can be transformed
into nouns and attached to persons, including bores, crooks, cuckolds, and
whores. The relevant task for our purposes is to distinguish between this
kind of resolution of challenge and those in which the outcome is negative
and interaction chokes to a stop, as in meaninglessness. That is, we must
distinguish between discrepancies between original definition and act that
result in ordinary and expected deviance, on the one hand, and discrepancies which result in terminal disintegration on the other.

A rather different kind of violation is that which could not, under any
circumstances, have been anticipated according to a normative order,
which cannot be described by the normative order even *after* it occurs,
and for which the social system provides no label, response, or sanction.
These might be called extraordinary violations, because there are no
guidelines by which the membership can describe what happened during
the incident at all. There are few examples of this kind of violation, as can
be seen in the very difficulty we have in naming and communicating them.
"Affectlessness" is a psychological label for acts where no norm seems any
more or less relevant than any other norm; and "psychopathy" designates
acts that, when taken together, are not only inconsistent according to the
normative order, but unclassifiable as well. The latter behavior, often
called "anti-social" because it seems directed against other persons, would
more appropriately be called anti-definable from the point of view of other
(normatively governed) persons.[11] In the deviant case the act is unanticipated in fact, whereas in the anti-definable one, it cannot even be anticipated in principle. In the first, a partner is proferred a way of defining and
handling the violation, but in the second, he is left entirely to his own
devices, without an institutionalized "structure" (using the *interaction* as
the referent point) that would make his response to the violation as clear
and continuous as his definition of the violation itself.

As a property of definition, normatively "anticipatable" violations
can, of course, be thematic in that the actor is permitted to see them in his

---

[11] I am using psychopathy in the social rather than the clinical sense here, to
refer to relations between actors that are independent of their psychic makeup.

diagnoses of particular acts. Following this line in our case, we might say that the likelihood that appears as a component of innovation reflects a normatively governed—that is, definable according to social rules already in existence—violation. An act can, if it is covered by a normative order, be both deviant and likely at the same time, as can be observed in the routine enforcement activity characteristic of those parts of the social structure that members call weak.

Three of the five meaningless anomics reinvoke order. This is rather surprising, if one assumes that meaninglessness is most pernicious in its destruction of the components of definition. Nevertheless, a return to the orderly definitions of emergence comes out of a complete inability to make any assessments at all. This may be due to the emptiness of definition, not in spite of it, because the void serves to lower the sense-maintaining standards of the actor. If meaninglessness is pernicious, in that there is not a single definitional base for making activity sensible, it may work in favor of a return to definition rather than against it. The subject may accommodate to disruption here, because of his raw impression that he is not alone, but in a situation which, although not now a social enterprise, continues to resemble one sensorily, and so he treats anything at all as a legitimate, that is, orderly and emergent, normative base. The mere presence of verbal noise, stemming from another body in a sensory establishment, may serve as a reminder of what once was, and persuade the subject to adopt any set of standards as his own. "Brainwashing," for example, is a phenomenon in which the erasure of interpersonal support makes the actor susceptible to any normative influence whatsoever in an effort to regain some semblance of a relationship. "T Group" settings are less severe examples of this, in which the practitioners euphemistically call normative changes "unfreezing."[12]

That powerlessness precedes all types of anomie is hard to reason through. Some subjects stay in this phase, others change to meaninglessness and innovation, others return to order. Perhaps subjects first tend to attribute the causes of disruption to laboratory conditions rather than to the experimenter because these conditions are cited as novel and different several times when subjects are solicited and instructed. They are the

---

12 *See* Edgar H. Schein, "Interpersonal Communication, Group Solidarity, and Social Influence," *Sociometry*, (June, 1960), pp. 148-161; Peter McHugh, "Disintegration as a Requisite of Resocialization," *Social Forces*, (March, 1966); Matthew B. Miles, "On Temporary Systems," in M. Miles, ed., *Innovation in Education* (New York: Teachers College Press, 1964), pp. 437-491.

reason for being there in the first place. If this is the case, first-stage powerlessness is no more than an artifact of the test. Alternatively, powerlessness may be a device for removing the culpability of the other. In this circumstance the subject can avoid dealing with an unworthy partner, and is able to define himself and the experimenter as affiliated in a common quest. Following this, there are perhaps continuing discrepancies that make such a stratagem impossible, and the subject becomes enmeshed in another form of anomie. But this is so speculative that it is best left to further investigation.

Summary

Emergence predominates during orderly interaction. On the other hand, relativity predominates when order is challenged. This change probably results from the difference between behavior that is in accordance with assumptions and behavior that is not, in which case those assumptions must be assessed against the scene. An orderly interaction always contains preexisting assumptions which the participants document through the emergent course of the interaction. As discrepancies arise, however, these assumptions are thrown into doubt and rise to the surface. Actors resolve the doubt by assessing them against the immediate environment. We are implying here an original *modus operandi* of limited effort, where vague appearances permit goals and presumed consensus to go unchecked until subjects are confronted by discrepancy. Orderly social action, largely temporal in flavor, exhibits an economy of control because of the belief that purposes will come to pass.

Once the orienting definition is disrupted, behavior develops in several different ways; the challenge of disruption can either be resolved or, failing this, transform the action into anomie. Anomie itself has several aspects, denoted by various congeries of the components of relativity. In some cases, relativity disappears entirely; in others, it incorporates characteristics of the external conditions of action; in still others, it is distinctly *ad hominum* in meaning. Order is maintained, or disorder created, by varying the confluence of emergence and relativity.

Trends between order, disorder, emergence, and relativity are apparently quite volatile. On a descriptive level, different elements of order exist

in different phases of the interview, but we are without conceptual or empirical links between components. We can show trends, but cannot bridge
them, so the suggestions put forward above are emphatically speculative.

A few cautions should be mentioned here. First, coding reliability,
high enough with some training,[13] nevertheless requires great leaps of inference in some cases, so the interpretation of data must be carefully
considered.

Second, the flow of predominance should not be understood as a
description of all kinds of interaction. Subjects were instructed several
times, both when they were solicited and when they came for the interview, about what they could expect and what they should do.[14] These
instructions surely formulate much of the substance of emergent assumptions, and one might expect subjects to begin documenting them immediately. But in everyday life there are circumstances less well-defined
beforehand; "new" situations of social change, social mobility, and
the like would, of course, display less emergence and more relativity.
Similarly, there are more exhaustively specified interactions, in which
emergence would receive even greater emphasis, that sociologists call
routinization—certain elements of bureaucracy, secondary relations, and
long-term primary interaction. In the natural social world, predominance
would vary in proportion to the clarity of the interaction.

Finally, the number of cases is small, especially in the more detailed
breakdowns. This makes findings chancy as perfect reproductions of ordinary life. Because the goal of the investigation is to develop a set of explicit ideas for depicting the definition of the situation, however, this
drawback is probably justified. It would seem that emergence and relativity are empirically meaningful ideas for doing this, for they are present

---

[13] Agreement between two coders familiar with the ideas and protocols was .68.

[14] Martin Orne finds that the laboratory itself tends to create its own results,
because it successfully demands of subjects that their behavior incorporate what the
experimenter wanted all along. "On the Social Psychology of Psychological Experiments," *American Psychologist*, 17 (November, 1962). More recent investigations,
however, are less clear. *See* W. D. Ward and K. D. Sandvold, "Performance Expectancy as a Determinant of Actual Performance," *Journal of Abnormal and Social Psychology* 67 (1963), 293-295; Aaron Lewin and Gilda F. Eckstein, "Does Expectancy
Determine Performance?," *Journal of Experimental Social Psychology* (August,
1965), pp. 248-55. Deutscher points out that a subject's conformity to demand characteristics is less likely to occur when the investigator's purposes cannot be derived
from the instructions. Irwin Deutscher, "Words and Deeds: Social Science and Social
Policy," *Social Problems* (Winter, 1966), pp. 235-254.

when situations are being defined. Further, these data indicate they are *important* to order, because they are absent when situations are without meaning, and change in amount and kind when situations are otherwise anomic. With modifications, our original concepts are borne out in the laboratory, and we can account for our observations by using them.

VIII

Conclusion

I have tried to describe the definition of the situation as one parameter of common-sense action. To portray a parameter is to depict what defining a situation is, rather than to explicate and distinguish the contents of various particular definitions; to be descriptive is to make an account of what it is, rather than to explain why it is what it is; and to study common-sense action is to use as materials what actors themselves are doing in the creation of their own milieux.

With regard to parameters, I have attempted to show that although different actors may construct substantively different particular definitions, they proceed by invoking the same devices, mechanisms, and so on, and this leads to recognizable contours of definition even among subjects who are talking about grossly different things. Here an expressed definition is the result of translating content into a set of *procedures* actors use to develop a relationship between experimenter and subject, a relation that then comes to be embodied in the subject's comments. The text of a definition, its content, arises out of the pretext of two domains of experience, emergence and relativity, which colonize the particular meanings that subjects each experience during the interaction. We have not tried to show that a student will define going on to college as a great sacrifice for himself and his family, or that a daughter will say that her mother wants to remarry. Rather, it has been our purpose to suggest, first, the conditions of meaning under which such choices come to be considered at all; second, how those conditions make the world *transparent* for the actor, that is, their service to content as they come to be invoked by him; and third, how they modify or sustain such choices during the backward-forward-sideways course of interaction.

If we interpret emergence and relativity as merely technical rules rather than basic ones, in that they indicate no more than useful means for attaining the end of given substantive definitions of the situation, we are led to the view that they may be replaced by any others that actors take to be more conducive to those meanings (continuing as psychotherapy, etc.), and are put squarely back in the muddle of variable meaning. However, as soon as it is seen (empirically, in terms of the changes in definition that occur in the face of laboratory surprise) that the substantive meanings themselves are defined by invoking the basic procedural rules of emergence and relativity, it becomes clear that such a view is untenable. We cannot speak of "change" in the basic rules of emergence and relativity in the same sense we speak of "change" in the substance of definition, and this is an implication of any parameter. We have been concerned more with how than what, with procedure more than content.

Furthermore, a concern with "how" questions is a descriptive tactic as distinguished from the "why" that guides explanatory work. Description and analysis, of course, are not mutually exclusive (and cannot be if they are at all general), but they do distinguish emphasis.[1] Because the theoretical status of emergence and relativity is not very firm, we have simply observed whether they hold any potential status at all. We have identified a set of laboratory interactions and how they can be used to depict the definition of the situation, not why they lead to it; what it is, not why it is. There were analyses, but these were meant to facilitate description more than the other way around, to depict the processes whereby one kind of act appears among and between others. By having used order and disorder as test conditions, we have been able to follow definition through them as a course of interaction, and to note changes as we go. So we have been engaged in more than simple classification, where one thing is separated from another by naming its special properties. Our description was a sequel to the naturalism of reporting and the nominalism of classification.

Moving on to common sense, Popper provides a useful introduction to the idea by distinguishing between natural and normative law.[2] The

---

[1] Brown states that the difference between explanation and description corresponds to the difference between providing reasons for an occurrence and depicting the way it took place, respectively. Robert Brown, *Explanation in Social Science*, p. 24.

[2] Karl Popper, *The Open Society and Its Enemies*, Vol. I (Princeton: Princeton University Press, 1963), pp. 57-59. For certain correctives of the assumption that the distinction resides in the immutability of natural laws, see Thomas Kuhn, *The Structure of Scientific Revolutions*.

latter can be changed by human fiat, the former cannot. A natural law is some statement that describes a phenomenon for those governed by paradigms in the physical sciences. For those so governed, the law itself cannot be changed merely because humans want to change it (although humans can, of course, modify the consequences of phenomena within its purview). But normative law, being man-made, can be changed merely by doing so: "If men define situations as real, they are real in their consequences." The critical distinction, for our purposes, is implied by the statement that men can change the law in one case but not in the other: Men both make and describe one kind of law, but only describe the phenomena of the other. Man, himself, imputes his history, whether it be of a nation, an economy, or an interaction and can affect its course in so doing; physical objects cannot. In one case, men are their own subjects, in the other they are not. The investigator in physical science is not confronted with what his objects of investigation make of something, because these objects do not make anything of anything. The scientist's version of an affair is the only one that need be sought. In social science, however, the possibility that the subjects of study will impute one thing at Time 1 and another at Time 2, and change their behavior accordingly, makes it imperative that we observe the process of imputation itself. In the one case, meaning (imputation) is totally a province of the scientist, in the other it belongs to both the scientist and his subjects. Thus, our scientific endeavor is to study the endeavors of common-sense social action—in our scene, these two endeavors are going on simultaneously.[3] From this we can draw several elemental points:

1. Being imputed, no social object is intrinsically meaningful.

2. Therefore, any object can, in principle, be defined in at least two ways.

3. The social scientist is only substituting for the actor when he presumes the actor will define an object in a particular way, for there are at least two definitions possible for the actor. Though he may be accurate

---

[3] These endeavors are less distinctive than I have had to make them seem here for purposes of explication. To illuminate the difference between physical and social objects, note how peculiar it would seem to call the behavior of atoms or trees an "endeavor." The reader might be interested in comparing these ideas and those to follow—in fact, the orientation of the whole study—with what has come to be called Ethnomethodology. See the works cited elsewhere by Harold Garfinkel, Aaron Cicourel, and Harvey Sacks.

or not in doing so, the antiscientific character of substitution resides in
the fact that we have no way of telling.[4]

4. Because it is antiscientific to study behavior by substitution, it is
no more than any other common-sense endeavor.

In sum, men-on-the-street create their own versions of their affairs,
and these versions exert influence; because they are man-made and can
change, they are problematic; because they are problematic, we cannot
take them for granted in accounting for social action.

It is not being proposed that social behavior is not amenable to scientific study, nor that we should restrict ourselves to mere sensitive delineations of social life. There is no *a priori* reason to suppose that we cannot
develop natural laws about normative laws. Yet we resist making the definitions of actors problematic, because such a position is equated with the
actor's point of view, and his point of view is supposed to have two drawbacks: First, it requires techniques that are antiobjective, such as role-
taking on the part of the investigator, and, second, his point of view also
becomes the point of view of the investigator. These are assertions that
certain features of life are not amenable to science, and make strange
bedfellows indeed of those who, although for very different reasons,
adopt this same position.

Such a position stems from the common acceptance of a very old and
questionable dichotomy between mind and body, thinking and doing, acting and behaving, indiscernibles and discernibles, the intellect and the
senses. It is a dichotomy which finds ready sociological expression in our
distinctions between theory and method, concept and datum, deduction
and induction. These distinctions in turn have forced us to view some
substantive matters as private, that is, as lurking but unobservable wisps
not suited to professions of empiricism. The private-public dualism has
itself created a mind side, replete with unobservables beyond the pale.

But need this be so? Could we, by rejecting the privacy principle,
open up the unobservable and, at the same time, retain our scientific purposes? I think so, if we can show that nothing of interest to us is private
and hence unobservable.

---

[4] That substitution is even possible we must attribute to the phylogeny of social
scientists and their subjects; that it occurs at all we might attribute to the seductions
of that state. It is yet another difference between the problems facing social and
physical scientists.

The most pointed discussions of privacy in sociology revolve around putting oneself in the place of the other. This issue takes two forms.[5]

1. The proper and necessary means of knowing the sensations, thoughts, and definitions of another is to feel that person's sensations, think his thoughts, define his definitions.

2. Anyone who has a sensation, a thought, or a definition *knows* that he has it because he feels it, thinks it, and defines it; and whatever can be known to exist by being felt, thought, or defined cannot be known to exist in any other way.

It is curious that each of these versions corresponds to a school in sociology. Those who elect the first premise tend to be introspectionists, and favor doing what is required by the premise. They accept the private and then say, "I want to know about this. My subject's definitions being private, the only procedure is for me to define his definitions too, and I am willing to adopt this procedure." Those who elect the second premise, on the other hand, are the positivists broadly defined, and favor not doing what is required by the premise. They also accept the private, but they say, "We cannot know the other's definitions, because knowing requires having, and I am unwilling to adopt this procedure." Each premise offers us the private parallel to the mind-body dichotomy; one group is seduced by it, the other repelled.

The first premise, in which I must think the thoughts of the other to understand him, presupposes that I can identify a thought *I* think as *his*. But how can this be done? If I think it, it is mine. The introspectionist version confuses the designation of ownership of material against non-material things. We may well sensibly distinguish his cars or coats from mine, but how can we think a thought and say it "belongs" to anyone else? We don't "possess" sensations, thoughts, and definitions the way we possess cars and coats. By acceding to the idea of privacy, and then maintaining that we can locate and designate the private of the other through the private of ourselves, introspectionists appropriate the material notion of ownership to the nonmaterial one. It is a false analogy, however, because the nonmaterial cannot be possessed or located in the same way. A role cannot, for example, be "seen" in the same way as an automobile—it

---

[5] These forms are slight paraphrases of Cook's. *See* John W. Cook, "Wittgenstein on Privacy," *Philosophical Review*, LXXIV (1965), pp. 281-314. *See also* J. L. Austin, "Other Minds," in Flew, ed., *Logic and Language*, pp. 342-388.

cannot be misplaced or sold. To think what the other is thinking is merely to have one's own thoughts, and provides no empirical leverage for the sociologist.

The second premise, another mode of privatism, is usually the justification for avoiding, on methodological grounds, the definitions, thoughts, and sensations of others. Because the only way to know them is to have them, they are to be skirted as unobservable. The important question, however, is whether having the rules, definitions, and sensations of life is the only way to know them. Alternatively, in what sense are they public? Are pains, hopes, disappointments, and maxims to be conceived as private modes of action?

Suppose for a moment that they are. What would be the result? If the only way to know them is to have them, they *could never be passed on.* How could something so entirely private as to require having before knowing ever be passed on? Incredibly, this premise makes socialization impossible. Those who are yet to have them could never have them, could never learn. Each society would die aborning, truly a Hobbesian jungle! There is apparently something public about the private.

The error here is the general error of privatism, namely, that we must know *his* feeling, when all we need to know is *what* he is feeling. It is not that we have his definition X, but that we know definition X, which he also knows. It is not something that we are both knowing and having, but something that we are only knowing. Possession is not ten-tenths of the rule. If it were, we could never be *mistaken,* never think we were tasting chocolate when it's mocha, or that she loved us when we were infatuated. We could never have any doubts at all. For possession of the thought, sensation, or definition would be all there was to it and would rule out the idea of mistake, of a test against circumstances. To be entirely private would obviate the possibility of a test, of tentativeness, of a change in mind; there would be nothing against which we could proceed because definitions would be permanently sealed in by their very existence.

The public displays of rules and definitions are themselves rules and definitions, not surface effluvia of private essences. Definitions are not owned, if by that we mean they are ineluctably private property, hidden away in the recesses of mind and self. They are *performances,* applied and validated, and thus public and observable:

1. *Of course* I *don't* introspect Tom's feelings. (We should be in a pretty predicament if I did.)

2. *Of course* I *do* sometimes know Tom is angry. Hence

3. To suppose that the question, "How do I know that Tom is angry?" is meant to mean, "How do I introspect Tom's feelings?" (because, as we know, that's the sort of thing knowing is or ought to be), is simply barking up the wrong gum tree.[6]

We need not replace the actor with ourselves by putting ourselves in his place—the previous argument illustrated the inadequacy of this—we need only know what he makes of his place. Just as there is no *a priori* reason to assume that social life cannot be scientifically studied, neither is there any apparent circumstance that obviates the scientific study of his point of view. This work attempts to develop one. Second, knowledge of this view in no way *restricts* us to it. To know the actor's rules is not to be limited by them, because we can do anything we please with these rules, including the creation of our own "hard" ones for dealing with his. We need only accrue our conceptualizations out of his, because his are both variable and influential and, therefore, must be explained.

In the final few pages, I shall use the distinction between physical and social metrics, and the actor's version of things, to translate chronological time into social time.

We alluded to "experience" before and I would like to specify that term with regard to the passage of events in social time. I will suggest that emergence and relativity can be used to depict social, as opposed to chronological, passage—that these are different metrics and, hence, the relations between them are problematic.

To begin, let us return again to "If men define situations as real, they are real in their consequences." That statement depicts the influence of definition on behavior, in that the meaning imputed to an object will influence behavior toward it. It implies a great deal more when we add serial courses of action: Changes in definition will be accompanied by changes in consequence. If we show that serial changes in definition do not occur in one-to-one relation to changes in chronology, we obviate the possibility of substituting one metric for the other.

Remember that emergence is an activity that predominates in orderly interaction, and is a documentation of theme that joins discrete events (say yeses and noes) through the anticipation of what *will* occur in the future (that the problem will be clarified), and the reconstruction of what *has* occurred in the past (that an ambiguous answer is now sensible in

_____

[6] *Ibid.*, p. 380.

light of greater information). This documentation, which at the time the comment is being made is occurring in the chronological present, resides in the *social*, that is definitional, past and future. When we refer to chronological time, subjects are behaving in the chronological present, to be sure, but the *social* action is circumscribed by the way events are conceived to have fallen in the past and the way they are expected to fall in the future. Socially speaking, an orderly event in the chronological present is pawn, absorbed by the previous flow of interaction and its expected future course. The status of the clock is contingent on definitions of past and future, for it is from these that it draws its character.

When order is overcast by disruption, and emphasis shifts to relative assessment of the environment, past and future procedures of definition give way to a consideration of the immediate locale. Emergent assumptions now become fugitive, the penumbrae of discrepancy, and must be authenticated, modified, dissolved. But how is this to be done? Everything was orderly in the past, so to rehearse it would be inappropriately redundant. And emergence binds the future to the past, leaving the future similarly empty of account.

Instead, subjects turn to what we have called social space, a relative mise-en-scene, a *social* present that changes the meaning of events in the *chronological* past and future. One subject, for example, decided in C5 that A5 means "He wants me to continue in school." Following withdrawal of his definition of the experiment as psychotherapy, he says in C8 that "Now I see . . . He's lying. He doesn't care whether I go on to school or not." The phrase "Now I see" is the outcome of the relative assessment that changes in the social *present* the meaning attributed to C5, the chronological place of which is the *past*. The meaning of the current discrepancy, and then withdrawal, recreated the event as it occurred in chronological time. Relativity, the social present, transformed A5 from "He wants" to "He doesn't care." Emergence, originally the habitat of A5, gives way to the relative present, where A5 undergoes a harsh purification of its original self.

Emergence and relativity are thus two faces of a dialectic. They operate in tandem, but not concurrently. The tentative agnosticism of surprise leads to an emphasis on immediate arrangements in the environment, the *social* present, and out of this assessment comes a change in the meaning of events in the *chronological* past. Order, on the other hand, deemphasizes the chronological present in favor of the linkage of events through the social past and toward the future. During order, that is, events to be defined in the *chronological* present exist in the *social* (emergent) past and future. During disorder, the meaning that resides in the chronological past and future is discovered in the social (relative) present. It is a harlequin design that is less metaphorical than chronology, because it is closer to the actual rhythm of definition and its consequences. Social time does not appear on the face of a clock, but Proust would have recognized it, and so would the actor of everyday life.

well,
a little
burst of style!

Index